Spelling Stations Teacher's Guide

Written by Abigail Steel and Lisa Holt

Download a **free map** to track your progress from:

www.letterland.com/information/downloads

Published by Letterland International Ltd,
Leatherhead, Surrey, KT22 9AD, UK
www.letterland.com

ISBN: 978-1-78248-3007
Product Code: TK23

© Letterland International Ltd 2018
LETTERLAND® is a registered trademark of Lyn Wendon.

10 9 8 7 6 5 4 3 2 1

Written by: Abigail Steel and Lisa Holt
Designed by: Lisa Holt and Laura Bittles

Originator of Letterland: Lyn Wendon

Sassoon Infant is a typeface designed for children learning to read and write. © Adrian Williams Design Ltd

The author asserts the moral right to be identified as the author of this work.

Any educational institution that has purchased one copy of this book may make duplicate copies of the Spelling Games for use exclusively within that institution. Permission does not extend to reproduction, storage within a retrieval system, or transmittal in any form or by any means, electronic, mechanical, photocopying, recording or otherwise, or duplicate copies for loaning, renting or selling to any other institution without the prior written permission of the Publisher or a licence permitting restricted copying in the United Kingdom issued by the Copyright Licensing Agency Ltd, 90 Tottenham Court Road, London W1T 4LP. This book is sold subject to the condition that it shall not by way of trade or otherwise be lent, hired out, sold, or otherwise circulated without the Publisher's written consent.

A catalogue record for this book is available from the British Library.

Printed and bound in India by Gopsons Papers Ltd.

Contents – Platform One

Introduction 4-10

Week 1 - Hill Pass
- **ff**, **ll** /f/ /l/ 12
- **ss**, **zz** /s/ /z/ 13

Week 2 - Dock King
- **ck** /k/ 16
- **k** /k/ 17

Week 3 - Glove Catch
- **-ve** 20
- **-tch** 21

Week 4 - Foxes Family
- Adding **s** and **es** to words 23
- **-y** /ee/ 24

Week 5 - Pink Picnic
- The /**ng**/ sound spelt **n** before **k** 27
- Division of words into syllables 28

Week 6 - Kicking Player
- Adding –**ing** to verbs 30
- Adding –**er** to verbs 31

Week 7 - Stopped Longer
- Adding –**ed** to verbs 34
- Adding –**er** to adjectives 35

Week 8 - The Quickest
- Tricky Words 38
- Adding –**est** to adjectives 39

Week 9 - Rainy Way
- **ai** 41
- **ay** 42

Week 10 - Lake Scene
- **a_e** 44
- **e_e** 45

Week 11 - Bike Zone
- **i_e** 47
- **o_e** 48

Week 12 - Huge Sheep
- **u_e** 50
- **ee** 51

Week 13 - Beach Head
- **ea** /ee/ 53
- **ea** /e/ 54

Week 14 - Field Farm
- **ie** /ee/ 56
- **ar** 57

Week 15 - Herb Dinner
- **er** (stressed) 59
- **er** (unstressed schwa) 60

Week 16 - Girls Surf
- **ir** 62
- **ur** 63

Week 17 Cool Book
- **oo** long /oo/ 65
- **oo** short /oo/ 66

Week 18 - Toad Toes
- **oa** 68
- **oe** 69

Week 19 - Snow House
- **ow** /oa/ 71
- Tricky Words 72

Week 20 - Loud Town
- **ou** 74
- **ow** /ou/ 75

Week 21 - Blue Crew
- **ue** long /oo/ 77
- **ew** long /oo/ 78

Week 22 - New Statue
- **ew** /yoo/ 80
- **ue** /yoo/ 81

Week 23 - Tie Bright
- **ie** /igh/ 83
- **igh** 84

Week 24 - Royal Soil
- **oy** 86
- **oi** 87

Week 25 - Short Shore
- **or** 89
- **ore** 90

Week 26 - Naughty Hawk
- **au** 92
- **aw** 93

Week 27 - Airport Near
- **air** 95
- **ear** /ear/ 96

Week 28 - Share Pears
- **are** /air/ 98
- **ear** /air/ 99

Week 29 - Dolphin Whistle
- **ph** 101
- **wh** 102

Week 30 - Unusual Sunset
- **un-** 104
- Compound words 105

Appendices 107-128

Introduction

Spelling in the English language is notoriously difficult to master. The reason for its complexity is the way in which the language has developed. It has been formed over hundreds of years and involves the amalgamation and adoption of many words and spelling variations from other languages such as French, Latin and German. It is good to share this concept with children so they don't think that spelling difficulties are a reflection of their own ability.

Letterland Spelling Stations can be used with any curriculum, however, this guide covers the statutory requirements for Spelling in the National Curriculum for English at Key Stage 1, Year 1 (England).

Spelling is a two-step process

Step 1: Segmenting the sounds from beginning to end

Children hear, think or say aloud the word they wish to spell. Then they separate out the sounds within the word (this is called segmenting). For example, if children want to spell **snail**, they must hear the **s-n-ai-l** sounds separately from beginning to end. In a longer word they may syllable chunk the word first. This means breaking the word into larger chunks before the individual sounds are identified. For example, in the word **butterfly**, they may segment as **butt-er-fly** first and then **b-u-tt-er-f-l-y**.

Step 2: Knowing which letter patterns represent which sounds

Once children can identify the sounds in a word from beginning to end they must then decide which way to write those sounds. For example, in the word **snail**, children need to know that the /ai/ sound is spelt with the letters **ai** and not **ay**. In the word **butterfly** they need to know that there is a double **tt** for the /t/ sound, the letters **er** when they hear the /uh/ sound and a **y** for the /igh/ sound at the end. Knowing which letter patterns represent the sounds in words relies on children's experience of vocabulary and Word Banks.

There is no short cut to learning which way words are spelt. Children require lots of practice with Word Banks, looking at spelling patterns and putting the words into context. Learning about spelling rules helps children become more aware of when and why words are spelt the way they are.

Although there is no single magic answer to learning all the spelling rules, there are proven ways in which we can help.

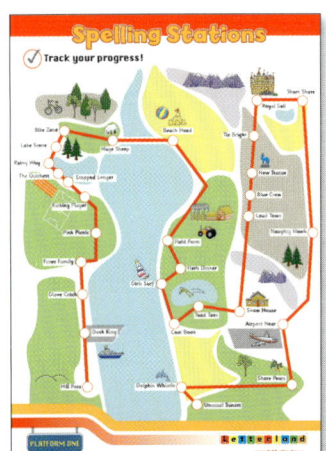

Research has shown that using a mnemonic system (an aide to memory) is a highly successful way of embedding spelling in children's long-term memory.

Letterland Spelling Stations uses several effective mnemonic strategies to embed spelling. The train station names provide an association for the linked banks of words and spelling rules. Each week has a station name and image associated with it. By remembering the station name, children have a visual clue to help them unlock the words of the week rather than simply having to remember an abstract list.

Download a **free map** of your journey to track your progress from:

www.letterland.com/information/downloads

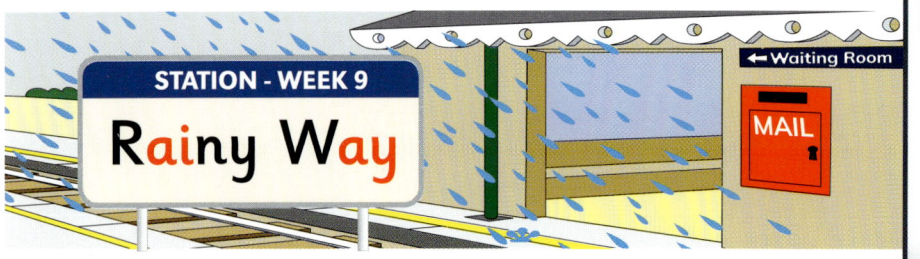

How to use *Letterland Spelling Stations*

Letterland Spelling Stations is designed to guide you step-by-step as you teach your children to spell. You can follow the lessons as they are or you can tailor the lessons to suit your children and your timetable.

Make the lessons engaging

To be able to spell confidently, children need to be able to recall which spelling patterns are in words. By making the lessons fun you will help to make learning memorable. It is therefore worth getting 'on board' with the theme of Spelling Stations in its entirety. You could put on a ticket inspector's hat at the start of each lesson and blow a whistle to show you are ready to start. You could even ask children to line up before the lesson and then board the train by taking their seats in the class.

A step-by-step approach

At the start of each lesson, **revise previous learning** by asking children to recall the rule, or some of the words, they learned about in the previous lesson. If they struggle you could support them by reminding them of the station name to prompt their memory. Don't spend too long on this but if you are concerned that the learning may not be embedded then make an observational note that you will need to return to the previous lesson for further consolidation or look to the other Letterland programmes, such as *Letterland Phonics* or *Letterland Grammar* to consolidate learning.

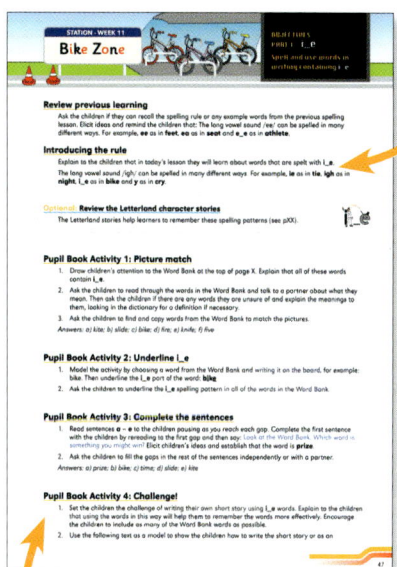

Next, move on to the lesson you are going to teach and introduce it by telling the children **the rule** and providing some examples.

Use the lesson plans to guide the children through the **activities** in the *Spelling Stations Pupil Book*. You may wish to divide the class, allowing more confident children to **work independently** through the activities (especially once they are familiar with the activity styles) while you focus your attention on supporting less confident children.

With a **supported group** you may wish to complete each activity in the *Pupil Book* as a whole group, providing detailed instruction for the children in the group to work at the same pace.

Always have a **dictionary** to hand to be able to provide accurate definitions of the vocabulary used in the lessons and any additional vocabulary that may be raised. Activities in the *Pupil Book* such as Picture Match and Complete the Sentences are designed to highlight the meanings of the words in the Word Bank.

Remind children to pay careful attention to the letters in the words. Activities like Underline (the spelling pattern), Complete the Sentences and Challenge! are designed to encourage children to notice and use the correct spellings.

You may wish to pause all the children at a mid-point in the lesson to discuss the answers of earlier activities in the *Pupil Book*. This can work well to identify any misconceptions that could be missed as the lesson progresses. Alternatively try to find some time towards the end of the lesson to review the activities and ask children to present to the class some of their answers in a collaborative feedback plenary.

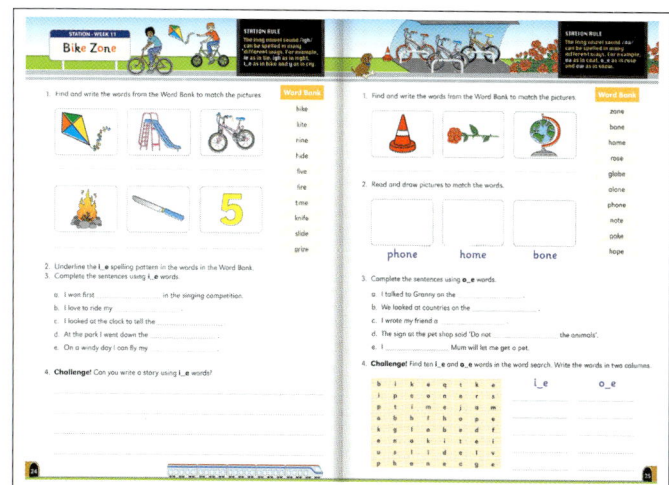

Teaching time: 2 x 30 minute sessions per week

The teaching week is divided into two parts. Each part should take around 20-30 minutes. Extension activities and optional games are provided that may extend the time somewhat if used. See pages 112-117.

Assessment

As part of your weekly routine (generally a Friday activity), spellings should be assessed. To stop this being 'the dreaded test', introduce the idea of **Spelling Stations!**

Each child should have a copy of *Spelling Stations Ticket Book - Platform One*. Each week they will be tested on the words from **one ticket**. Children will have covered the spelling patterns in class in their *Pupil Book*. Children should be encouraged to revise the spellings in the *Ticket Book* at home with a parent/carer.

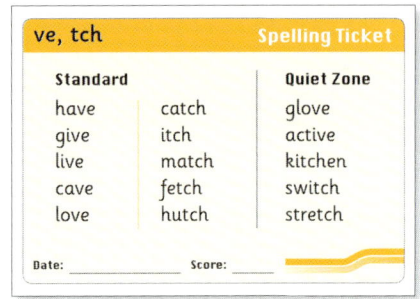

Teacher: At the start of the spelling test, you could say: **"Spelling Stations - Tickets Please!"** You could blow a whistle to signify the start and end of the test, or even put on a hat and pretend to be a ticket inspector.

Teacher: Collect in the *Spelling Stations Ticket Books*.

Teacher: Read out the 'Standard' Word Bank and sentences from the Assessment section of the *Teacher's Guide* to the children slowly. Repeat.

Students: Write their test answers in their own exercise book, or on a separate sheet of paper.

Teacher: Read out the five further 'Quiet Zone' words to spell for those in the class that need more of a spelling challenge. Remind the other children that they are in the 'Quiet Zone' and must stay quiet to help the other children concentrate.

Teacher: Collect all the student's answers to be marked.

(Option) Children can check their own answers against their *Ticket Books*.

Teacher: Mark the papers and keep a record of the spelling scores on the sheets provided or your own class record (pages 109-110).

Teacher: Fill in the date (or use a date stamp) in each child's *Ticket Book* and their score. Return marked Spelling Tests to your students. Ask them to look at any errors they have made and write those words again in the space provided **on the back of their Spelling Ticket** so they (and their parents) have a record of how they are getting on with their spellings.

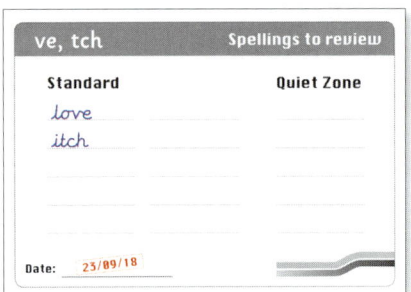

Extension Option

To extend the assessment activity and provide further challenge, you could use the sentences from the Assessment section for full sentence dictations by reading them slowly and pausing after every few words to give children time to write down the full sentences.

Differentiation

Children learn in different ways and develop at different paces. *Letterland Spelling Stations* addresses this by providing a range of aural, visual and kinaesthetic targeted spelling activities that embrace different learning styles. Differentiation opportunities are woven throughout so children are appropriately supported yet actively encouraged to stretch further. *Letterland Spelling Stations* is designed to be used with your whole class with built-in ways to accommodate below year group level spellers and students whose first language is not English, as well as those who are spelling above age-related expectations.

You will expect most students to learn the Standard list of 10 words per week, and the high achieving students to learn 15 words (both Standard and Quiet Zone). However you may discretely advise some students which portion of the list he or she is responsible for learning. For example, you could limit a student to only being expected to spell 5 Standard Words. They fully participate in class activities but are evaluated primarily on assigned words.

Vocabulary discussion is particularly useful for new English language children (ELL) with the following adaptations:

- Include discussion of word meanings for **all words**.
- Involve ELL students in providing examples and finishing sentence stems after a few native speakers have modelled this process for a particular word.
- Guide your students in finding words with the same meaning in their first language through online translation sites.
- Because many languages have roots in the same languages, cognates can be found that are similarly spelt or pronounced in English and other languages.
- For students who are well below age-related expectations in reading and spelling, intervention at their instructional level is important.

Games

There are some activities and games provided at the back of this guide (page 112-117). These are optional and can be used at any time to consolidate learning. Each game is 'train themed' so your class can really embrace the idea of Spelling Stations!

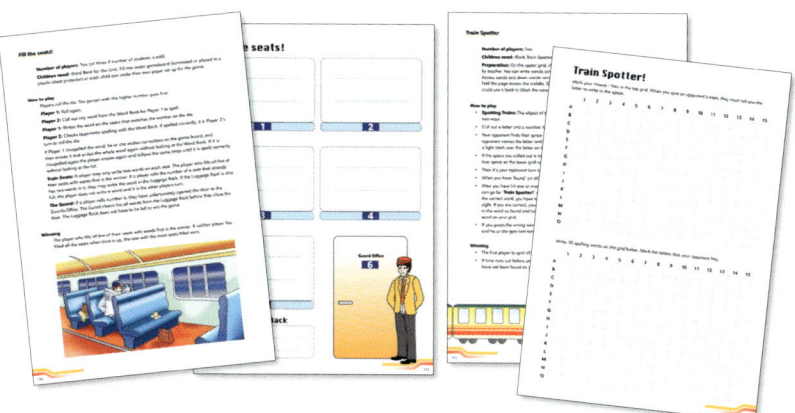

Full literacy support with Letterland

As a further source of reinforcement links are provided throughout the *Letterland Spelling Stations Teacher's Guide* to the *Letterland Phonics* character stories and the *Letterland Grammar* analogies.

Letterland covers all the curriculum requirements for literacy development including spelling, phonics and grammar. The resources we offer can be used independently of each other or together. **The uniting factor of all our materials is that the stories and analogies engage students leading to long term retention of concepts. Letterland is a child-friendly land of learning.**

For more information about *Letterland Phonics* or *Letterland Grammar*, see pages 118-127.

Pupil Resources

Spelling Stations Pupil Book - Platform One

Each child should have a copy of the *Spelling Stations Pupil Book*. The book contains 30 double-page spreads, equivalent to two 20 minute sessions of activities per week. It covers the statutory requirements for Spelling in the National Curriculum for English at Key Stage 1, Year 1 (England).

The *Pupil Books* provide children with a reminder of **the spelling rule** for the session and a collection of **activities** to consolidate learning. Some activities highlight the meanings of the words in the Word Bank, while others remind children to pay careful attention to the letters within those words.

Activities can be completed as a **whole class**, or as **independent work**.

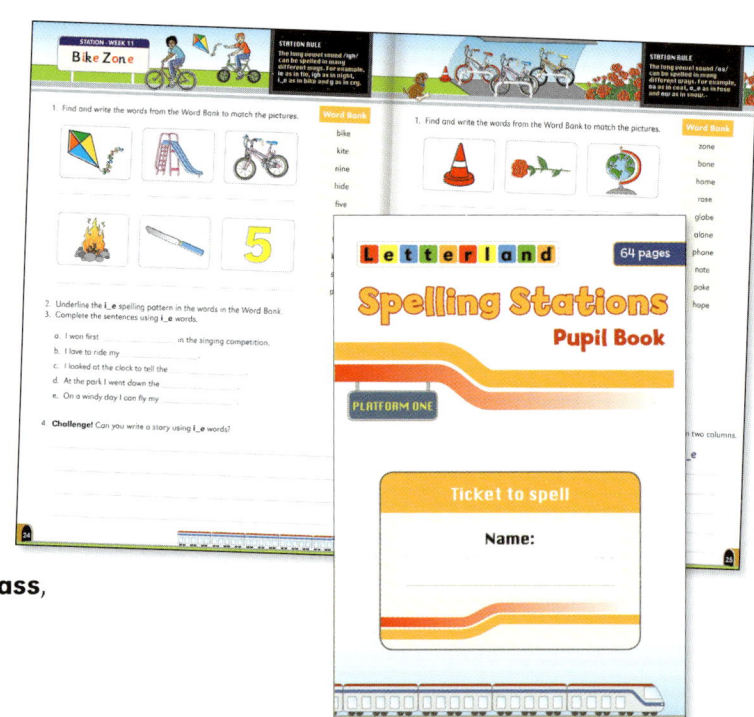

Spelling Stations Ticket Book - Platform One

Each child should have a copy of the *Spelling Stations Ticket Book*. The book contains all the Word Banks and spelling patterns they will learn throughout the year. It provides a collection of spelling knowledge to be kept and referred to as needed.

Each week children will be tested on the words from **one ticket**. Children will have covered the spelling patterns in class, and they should also be encouraged to revise the spellings in the *Spelling Stations Ticket Book* at home with a parent/carer.

The tickets provide a record of how each child is progressing with their spelling. Getting a ticket stamped each week by the teacher gives a real sense of accomplishment.

When all the tickets are stamped, your pupils will be ready to move forward on their spelling journeys!

Ticket Book - Word Bank

Standard - 10 words per week	Quiet Zone - 5 words per week
Words that exemplify applicable syllable or spelling patterns as outlined in the curriculum* Common exception 'tricky' words	Words of interest that spur further engagement with vocabulary for those children who need more of a challenge

*National Curriculum for England

Expanding vocabulary and understanding

Discussion in your classroom will depend upon your students' knowledge and needs. You may spend little time on words that children seem to fully understand and more time on words with more complex or multiple meanings. Here are some ideas you can use to guide and enhance understanding.

- Provide a child-friendly definition. If you **pause** (Week 26) you stop for a while, then carry on.
- Say a sentence with context clues and let children infer the meaning. The boy **paused** the TV programme while he went to the toilet.
- Compare the word to other words. If I **pause** I don't stop it or end it.
- Use the word in different contexts. Let's take a **pause**. Press the **pause** button. I waited for a **pause** in the conversation.
- Provide additional meanings of the word if there are any. Talk about homophones (words that sound the same but have different spellings and meaning) e.g. **pause / paws**.

Week	Focus	Standard	Quiet Zone
1	ff ll ss zz	off, puffin hill, bell, doll miss, fuss, dress jazz, buzz	daffodil, stuff, gruff blossom frizz
2	ck k	duck, pack, clock, kick, sock kid, skin, kitten, kiss, kit	rocket, quick, brick, kettle, napkin
3	-ve -tch	have, give, live, olive, love catch, itch, match, fetch, hutch	glove, active kitchen, switch, stretch
4	-s, -es -y /ee/	cats, pens, hats, foxes, buses happy, muddy, sunny, family, grumpy	chats, watches funny, silly, dirty
5	-nk 2 syllables	bank, think, sunk, pink, honk rabbit, carrot, pocket, robot, picnic	drink, thank thunder, robin, salad
6	-ing -er	jumping, singing, barking, sailing, kicking painter, farmer, helper, player, gardener	spending, telling, hunting, singing, banker
7	-ed -er	melted, lifted, rested, locked, sorted shorter, lower, quicker, slower, colder	talked, watched, opened taller, warmer
8	Tricky Words -est	said, are, you, today, was freshest, fastest, strongest, weakest, grandest	were, your, they youngest, brightest
9	ai ay	rain, wait, train, paid, aim day, play, stay, clay, away	afraid, chain crayon, holiday, spray

Week	Focus	Standard	Quiet Zone
10	a_e e_e	cake, case, rake, gate, cave these, theme, athlete, compete, delete	stale, grape, spade trapeze, concrete
11	i_e o_e	five, bike, kite, nine, hide cone, rose, home, globe, bone	prize, knife, slide phone, broke
12	u_e ee	rude, tune, flute, cube, June sheep, green, three, sleep, bee	brute, plume agree, knee, teeth
13	ea /ee/ ea /e/	sea, leaf, peach, seal, bean bread, read, head, thread, instead	please, season, reach ahead, dread
14	ie /ee/ ar	field, thief, chief, piece, movie star, car, shark, March, park	shield, mischief garden, market, harvest
15	er (stressed) er (unstressed)	herb, person, mermaid, term, her teacher, winter, summer, under, sister	alert, nerve mother, flower, brother
16	ir ur	girl, bird, shirt, first, third turn, hurt, church, burst, Thursday	birthday, circus, thirst injured, surprise
17	oo /long oo/ oo /short oo/	food, pool, moon, zoo, spoon book, took, foot, wood, good	balloon, tooth, proof mistook, stood
18	oa oe /oa/	boat, coat, road, coach, goal toe, doe, oboe, aloe, woe	throat, coast potatoes, tomatoes, volcanoes
19	ow /oa/ Tricky Words	own, blow, snow, grow, arrow here, there, where, come, one	below, rainbow, pillow friend, house
20	ou ow /ou/	out, about, mouth, around, sound crown, towel, frown, owl, gown	pound, flour brow, scowl, howl
21	ue /oo/ ew /oo/	blue, clue, true, glue, cruel grew, flew, drew, threw, chew	gruesome, clueless screws, jewels, cashew
22	ew /yoo/ ue /yoo/	new, few, knew, stew, nephew rescue, Tuesday, argue, barbecue, queue	skewer, mildew value, statue, overdue
23	ie /igh/ igh	lie, tie, pie, cried, tried high, night, light, bright, right	magpie, necktie sigh, knight, flight
24	oy oi	boy, toy, enjoy, annoy, joy oil, join, coin, point, soil	enjoyed, annoyed toilet, joint, avoid
25	or ore	fork, short, born, horse, morning more, score, tore, wore, shore	important, story, sword before, chore
26	au aw	author, pause, haul, autumn, sauce saw, draw, yawn, crawl, jaw	August, dinosaur, astronaut shawl, squawk
27	air ear /ear/	air, fair, pair, hair, chair dear, hear, beard, near, year	dairy, repair, upstairs shears, earrings
28	are /air/ ear /air/	bare, dare, care, share, spare bear, pear, wear, tear, swear	scared, aware, square early, earth
29	ph wh	dolphin, alphabet, elephant, phone, trophy when, where, which, wheel, while	orphan, typhoon white, whisper, whistle
30	un- compound words	unhappy, undo, unload, unfair, unlock football, farmyard, sunset, rainbow, toothbrush	unafraid, unblock playground, blackberry, butterfly

Step-by-Step Lesson Plans

STATION - WEEK 1

Hill Pass

OBJECTIVES
PART 1 – ff and ll
Spell and use words in writing containing ff and ll

Introducing Letterland Spelling

At the start of each lesson you will review previous learning. As this is the very first Letterland Spelling lesson, ask the children to think about whether they always spell words with the correct letters. Elicit ideas and establish that spelling in English is very difficult because we have multiple ways of writing some sounds, for example there are nine different ways to spell the /ai/ sound (**ai**, **ay**, **a**, **a-e**, **ea**, **ae**, **eigh**, **aigh**, **ey**). Reassure the children that over time they will learn how to spell correctly using the *Letterland Spelling Stations*, and that it will be great fun!

Introducing the rule

NOTE: Each lesson has a **rule**. Within this guide we use the terms **consonants** and **long** and **short vowels**. It is important that children understand these terms so check this at the very start of your first lesson. Some children find describing sounds as 'long' or 'short' as quite a difficult concept. They benefit from having a visual prompt with ideational content which can then become their recall route if they forget which is which. *Letterland Phonics* (see page 120) provides child-friendly characters and stories to associate with vowels to prevent any confusion.

Explain to the children that in today's lesson they will learn about words that are spelt with **ff** and words that are spelt with **ll**.

The sounds /f/ and /l/ are usually spelt as **ff** and **ll** if they come straight after a single vowel (short vowel sounds), for example: co**ff**ee, she**ll**.

Optional: Review the Letterland character stories

Letterland stories help children to remember these spelling patterns (see page 120).

Hand out a copy of the *Spelling Stations Pupil Book* to each child. Explain that each week they will complete two pages of the book. At first, this will be done as a **whole class activity**, but as time progresses, some of this work may be done in **small groups** or **independently**.

Pupil Book Activity 1: Picture Match

1. Draw children's attention to the Word Bank at the top of page 2. Explain that all of these words contain either **ff** or **ll**.
2. Ask the children to read through the words in the Word Bank and talk to a partner about what they mean. Then ask the children if there are any words they are unsure of and explain the meanings to them, looking in the dictionary for a definition if necessary.
3. Ask the children to find and copy words from the Word Bank to match the pictures.
   Answers: a) puffin; b) cuff; c) shell; d) bell; e) doll; f) coffee

Pupil Book Activity 2: Underline ff and ll

1. Model the activity by choosing a word from the Word Bank and writing it on the board, for example: **off**. Then underline the **ff** (or **ll**) part of the word: o**ff**.
2. Ask the children to underline the **ff** and **ll** spelling pattern in all of the words in the Word Bank. Ask: Does the **ff** and **ll** pattern always come at the end of the words? (No, see **coffee** and **puffin**).

Pupil Book Activity 3: Circle the Vowel

1. Ask the children to tell you what the vowel letters are (**a**, **e**, **i**, **o**, **u**). Remind the children of the spelling rule – that a word is usually spelt with **ff** and **ll** if it comes after single vowel letter.
2. Ask the children to go back through the words in the Word Bank and this time use a coloured pen or pencil to circle the vowel letter that comes before the **ff** and **ll** patterns. Ask the children to read the words and listen carefully to check if the vowel letter represents a short vowel sound.

Pupil Book Activity 4: Complete the Sentences

1. Read sentences **a** – **e** to the children, pausing as you reach each gap. Complete the first sentence with the children by re-reading to the first gap and then say: Look at the Word Bank. Which word is something you might find on the beach? Elicit children's ideas and establish that the word is **shell**.
2. Ask the children to fill in the gaps in the rest of the sentences independently or with a partner. *Answers: a) shell; b) puffin, cliff; c) doll; d) coffee; e) bell*

Pupil Book Activity 5: Challenge!

Set the children the challenge of writing their own short story using **ff** and **ll** words. Explain to the children that using the words in this way will help them to remember the words more effectively. Encourage the children to include as many of the Word Bank words as possible.

Use the following text as a model to show the children how to write the short story or, alternatively, use the text as a passage dictation by reading each sentence slowly and clearly for the children to write down:

Jill went to the beach with her sister. She saw puffins on the cliff. She found a shell on the beach. She climbed a hill and saw a wishing well. Jill wished for a new doll.

Watch Out!

Draw the children's attention to the Watch Out! box at the bottom of the page. Ask the children to read out the words: **tall**, **small**, **call**, **ball**.

Ask the children to talk with a partner and then tell you what vowel sound they can hear in these words. Elicit ideas and establish that the vowel sound is an /or/ (regional dialects may alter the sound slightly).

Tell the children that there are some words, like these, that have **ll** but do not have a short vowel sound before those letters.

Optional: Review the Letterland story

To help, you might like to talk about Giant All, who lives in Letterland and steals all the apples!

Exceptions to the rule include: **if**, **pal**

Review previous learning

Ask the children if they can recall the spelling rule or any example words from the previous spelling lesson. Elicit ideas and remind the children that: The sounds /f/ and /l/ are usually spelt as **ff** and **ll** if they come straight after a single vowel letter (short vowel sounds), for example: co**ff**ee, she**ll**.

Introducing the rule

Explain to the children that in today's lesson they will learn about words that are spelt with **ss** and with **zz**. The sounds /s/ and /z/ are usually spelt as **ss** and **zz** if they come straight after a single vowel letter ('short vowel' sounds), for example: dre**ss**, di**zz**y.

> **OBJECTIVES**
> **PART 2 – SS and ZZ**
> Spell and use words in writing containing **ss** and **zz**

Optional: Review the Letterland character stories
Letterland stories help children to remember these spelling patterns (see page 120).

Pupil Book Activity 1: Picture Match

1. Draw the children's attention to the Word Bank at the top of page 3. Explain that all of these words contain either **ss** or **zz**.
2. Ask the children to read through the words in the Word Bank and talk to a partner about what they mean. Then ask the children if there are any words they are unsure of and explain the meanings to them, looking in the dictionary for a definition if necessary.
3. Ask the children to find and copy words from the Word Bank to match the pictures.

Answers: a) buzz; b) press; c) dress

Pupil Book Activity 2: Word Match

1. Draw the children's attention to the words written underneath the blank drawing boxes.
2. Ask the children to read each word and talk to a partner about what they mean.
3. Ask the children to draw a simple picture to match the words underneath each box, for example, to match the word 'hiss', children could draw a snake that makes a hissing noise.

Pupil Book Activity 3: Complete the Sentences

1. Read sentences **a** – **e** to the children, pausing as you reach each gap. Complete the first sentence with the children by re-reading to the first gap and then say: Look at the Word Bank. Which word is something you might feel if you spin around? Elicit the children's ideas and establish that the word is **dizzy**.
2. Ask the children to fill in the gaps in the rest of the sentences independently or with a partner.
Answers: a) dizzy; b) frizz; c) jazz; d) press; e) fuss

Pupil Book Activity 4: Challenge!

1. Draw the children's attention to the Word Search at the bottom of page 3. Set children the challenge of finding ten **ss** and **zz** words in the Word Search. Eight of the words run horizontally from left to right and two words run vertically from top to bottom.
2. Tell the children to circle each word as they find it and then write the words in the correct column.

Answers:

p	u	z	z	l	e	f	f
d	m	i	s	s	g	d	r
b	u	z	z	i	l	r	i
e	m	h	i	s	s	e	z
n	j	a	z	z	j	s	z
f	u	s	s	b	k	s	c
h	o	p	d	i	z	z	y
a	r	t	g	l	a	s	s

ss	zz
miss	puzzle
hiss	frizz
fuss	buzz
glass	dizzy
dress	jazz

Think about it!

1. Ask the children to read the words in the Think about it! box: **class**, **pass**, **glass**, **brass**.

2. Ask them to think about how they pronounce the words and whether they have a short or long vowel sound.
3. Explain that depending on where they live some people may pronounce these words with a short /a/ sound and other people may pronounce them with an /ar/ sound. Reassure the children that both versions of pronunciation are correct.

Assessment Process

Hand out a copy of the *Spelling Stations Ticket Book* to each child.

Explain that this is *their* book of tickets and as with any ticket, it is very important that it isn't lost or damaged. Each week they will need to learn the spellings on **one ticket**. They can write the date on the ticket they need to learn (or you can date stamp it).

Encourage children to learn their weekly spelling ticket at home. There are strategies at the beginning of the *Ticket Book* to help guide parents/carers.

Full details of how to carry out assessment can be found on pages 6 and 108 of this guide.

Assessment: ff, ll, ss, zz

Tell the children that you are going to read out ten words, one at a time. Each word will be one of the **ff**, **ll**, **ss** or **zz** words that they have been learning. Tell the children that you will say the word, and then you will read out a sentence containing the word to help them know what it means. You will then repeat the word on its own before pausing so that the children can write the word down. For example: 1. **off**. I take the toy box lid **off**. **off**

1. **off**. I took the toy box lid **off**.
2. **miss**. I **miss** my mum when she is at work. **miss**
3. **puffin**. I have a toy **puffin**. **puffin**
4. **fuss**. My cat makes a **fuss**. **fuss**
5. **hill**. We climbed up the **hill**. **hill**
6. **dress**. My sister's **dress** has red stripes. **dress**
7. **bell**. I heard the **bell** ring. **bell**
8. **jazz**. We like to listen to **jazz** music. **jazz**
9. **doll**. We gave Poppy a new **doll**. **doll**
10. **buzz**. I heard the **buzz** of a bumblebee. **buzz**

For those students who need a bit more of a spelling challenge, read out the five further 'Quiet Zone' words to spell: **daffodil**, **stuff**, **gruff**, **blossom**, **frizz**.

STATION - WEEK 2

Dock King

OBJECTIVES
PART 1 – ck

Spell and use words in writing containing ck

Review previous learning

Ask the children if they can recall the spelling rule or any example words from the previous spelling lesson. Elicit ideas and remind the children that: The sounds /s/ and /z/ are usually spelt as **ss** and **zz** if they come straight after a single vowel letter (short vowel sounds), for example: dre**ss**, di**zz**y.

Introducing the rule

Explain to the children that in today's lesson they will learn about words that are spelt with **ck**.

The sound /k/ is usually spelt as **ck** if it comes straight after a single vowel letter (short vowel sounds), for example: du**ck**, pa**ck**

Optional: Review the Letterland character stories

The Letterland stories help children to remember this spelling pattern (see page 120).

Pupil Book Activity 1: Picture Match

1. Draw children's attention to the Word Bank at the top of page 4. Explain that all of these words contain **ck**.
2. Ask the children to read through the words in the Word Bank and talk to a partner about what they mean. Then ask the children if there are any words they are unsure of and explain the meanings to them, looking in the dictionary for a definition if necessary.
3. Ask the children to find and copy words from the Word Bank to match the pictures.
   Answers: a) clock; b) duck; c) sock; d) stick; e) lock; f) kick

Pupil Book Activity 2: Underline ck

1. Model the activity by choosing a word from the Word Bank and writing it on the board, for example: **clock**. Then underline the **ck** part of the word: clo**ck**.
2. Ask the children to underline the **ck** spelling pattern in all of the words in the Word Bank. Ask: Does the **ck** pattern always come at the end of the words? (No, see **ticket**, **rocket** and **jacket** at bottom of page 4)

Pupil Book Activity 3: Circle the Vowel

1. Ask the children to tell you what the vowel letters are (**a**, **e**, **i**, **o**, **u**). Remind the children of the spelling rule – that a word is usually spelt with **ck** if it comes after single vowel letter.
2. Ask the children to go back through the words in the Word Bank and this time use a coloured pen or pencil to circle the vowel letter that comes before the **ck** pattern. Ask the children to read the words and listen carefully to check if the vowel letter represents a short vowel sound.

Pupil Book Activity 4: Complete the Sentences

1. Read sentences **a** – **e** to the children, pausing as you reach each gap. Complete the first sentence with the children by re-reading to the first gap and then say: Look at the Word Bank. Which word is something you would do with a suitcase before going on a holiday? Elicit children's ideas and

establish that the word is **pack**.

2. Ask the children to fill in the gaps in the rest of the sentences independently or with a partner.

Answers: a) pack; b) duck; c) sock; d) kick; e) peck

Pupil Book Activity 5: Challenge!

1. Set the children the challenge of writing their own short story using **ck** words. Explain to the children that using the words in this way will help them to remember the words more effectively. Encourage the children to include as many of the Word Bank words as possible.

2. Use the following text as a model to show the children how to write the short story or, alternatively, use the text as a passage dictation by reading each sentence slowly and clearly for the children to write down:
Mum looked at the **clock**. It was time to put on my **socks** and shoes to go to the park. We walked up the **track**. I saw a **duck** on the pond. I ate an apple for my **snack**.

Watch Out!

1. Draw the children's attention to the Watch Out! box at the bottom of the page. Ask the children to read out the words: **ticket**, **rocket**, **jacket**.

2. Ask the children to talk with a partner and then tell you which part of these words is tricky to spell. Elicit ideas and establish that the end vowel sound is an /i/ but it is spelt with a letter **e**.

3. Tell the children that we need to try to remember that when we want to write these words that we use a letter **e** and not an **i**.

Additional teaching notes

4. At the beginning of many words the letter **c** is used for the /k/ sound (**c**at). The letter **k** is used before the letters **e**, and **i** (**k**ey, **k**ite).

5. In the middle of words the letters **ck** are used for the /k/ sound (po**ck**et).

6. At the end of words the letters **ck** are used after one short vowel sound (pa**ck**).

7. The letters **ke** are used after one long vowel sound (ma**ke**). The letter **k** is usually used after the letters **l**, **r** and **n** (mil**k**, wor**k**, thin**k**).

Review previous learning

Ask the children if they can recall the spelling rule or any example words from the previous spelling lesson. Elicit ideas and remind the children that: The sound /k/ is usually spelt as **ck** if it comes straight after a single vowel letter (short vowel sounds), for example: du**ck**, pa**ck**.

OBJECTIVES
PART 2 – k
Spell and use words in writing containing k

Introducing the rule

Explain to the children that in today's lesson they will learn about words that are spelt with **k**.

The sound /k/ is usually spelt as **k** if it comes before the letters **e** or **i**, for example: **k**ey, **k**ite.

Optional: Review the Letterland character stories

The Letterland stories help children to remember this spelling pattern (see page 120).

17

Pupil Book Activity 1: Picture Match

1. Draw the children's attention to the Word Bank at the top of page 5. Explain that all of these words contain **k**.
2. Ask the children to read through the words in the Word Bank and talk to a partner about what they mean. Then ask the children if there are any words they are unsure of and explain the meanings to them, looking in the dictionary for a definition if necessary.
3. Ask the children to find and copy words from the Word Bank to match the pictures.

Answers: a) skin; b) kitten; c) king

Pupil Book Activity 2: Word Match

1. Draw the children's attention to the words written underneath the blank drawing boxes.
2. Ask the children to read each word and talk to a partner about what they mean.
3. Ask the children to draw a simple picture to match the words underneath each box, for example, to match the word '**kiss**', children could draw themselves kissing a bedtime toy.

Pupil Book Activity 3: Complete the Sentences

1. Read sentences **a** – **e** to the children, pausing as you reach each gap. Complete the first sentence with the children by re-reading to the first gap and then say: Look at the Word Bank. Which word is the name for a baby goat? Elicit the children's ideas and establish that the word is **kid**.
2. Ask the children to fill in the gaps in the rest of the sentences independently or with a partner.

Answers: a) kid; b) skin; c) skip; d) kit; e) kite

Pupil Book Activity 4: Challenge!

1. Draw the children's attention to the Word Search at the bottom of page 5. Set children the challenge of finding ten **ck** and **k** words in the Word Search. Eight of the words run horizontally from left to right and two words run vertically from top to bottom.
2. Tell the children to circle each word as they find it and then write the words in the correct column.

Answers:

s	o	c	k	d	w	l	c
a	k	i	t	m	e	v	l
h	b	o	k	i	s	s	o
l	i	k	i	c	k	f	c
o	k	i	t	e	r	t	k
c	j	c	p	k	i	n	g
k	n	d	u	c	k	s	u
g	k	e	t	t	l	e	x

ck	k
sock	kit
clock	kiss
kick	kite
lock	king
duck	kettle

Think about it!

1. Ask the children to think about whether they have any friends whose names have a **k** spelling.
2. Elicit ideas and write any names they tell you on the board, for example, **Karen**, **Kevin**, **Kim**.

Assessment: ck, k

Tell the children that you are going to read out ten words, one at a time. Each word will be one of the **ck** or **k** words that they have been learning. Tell the children that you will say the word, and then you will read out a sentence containing the word to help them know what it means. You will then repeat the word on its own before pausing so that the children can write the word down. For example: 1. **duck**. The **duck** pecked the seeds. **duck**

1. **duck**. The **duck** pecked at the seeds. **duck**
2. **kid**. A baby goat is called a **kid**. **kid**
3. **pack**. I have a **pack** of cards. **pack**
4. **skin**. I have freckles on my **skin**. **skin**
5. **clock**. We looked at the time on the **clock**. **clock**
6. **kitten**. Our cat had a **kitten**. **kitten**
7. **kick**. I tried to **kick** the ball hard. **kick**
8. **kiss**. I **kiss** my teddy good night. **kiss**
9. **sock**. I lost one red **sock**. **sock**
10. **kit**. My football **kit** gets mud on it. **kit**

For those students who need a bit more of a spelling challenge, read out the five further 'Quiet Zone' words to spell: **rocket**, **quick**, **brick**, **kettle**, **napkin**

Full details of how to carry out assessment can be found on pages 6 and 108 of this guide.

STATION - WEEK 3
Glove Catch

OBJECTIVES
PART 1 –ve

Spell and use words in writing ending in -ve

Review previous learning

Ask the children if they can recall the spelling rule or any example words from the previous spelling lesson. Elicit ideas and remind the children that: The sound /k/ is usually spelt as **k** if it comes before the letters **e**, **i** or **y**, for example: **key, kid.**

Introducing the rule

Explain to the children that in today's lesson they will learn about words that have the /v/ sound **at the end**. The sound /v/ is usually spelt as **ve** if it comes at the end of a word, for example: ha**ve**, gi**ve**.

Optional: Review the Letterland character stories

Character-based stories can help children to remember spelling patterns (see page 120).

Pupil Book Activity 1: Picture Match

1. Draw the children's attention to the Word Bank at the top of page 6. Explain that all of these words contain **ve**.
2. Ask the children to read through the words in the Word Bank and talk to a partner about what they mean. Then ask the children if there are any words they are unsure of and explain the meanings to them, looking in the dictionary for a definition if necessary.
3. Ask the children to find and copy words from the Word Bank to match the pictures.

Answers: a) twelve; b) dove; c) glove

Pupil Book Activity 2: Word Match

1. Draw the children's attention to the words written underneath the blank drawing boxes.
2. Ask the children to read each word and talk to a partner about what they mean.
3. Ask the children to draw a simple picture to match the words underneath each box, for example, to match the word 'love', children could draw a heart or a close family member.

Pupil Book Activity 3: Complete the Sentences

1. Read sentences **a – e** to the children, pausing as you reach each gap. Complete the first sentence with the children by re-reading to the first gap and then say: *Look at the Word Bank. Which word is a number?* Elicit the children's ideas and establish that the word is **twelve**.
2. Ask the children to fill in the gaps in the rest of the sentences independently or with a partner.

Answers: a) twelve; b) olives; c) detective; d) live; e) dove

Pupil Book Activity 4: Challenge!

1. Set children the challenge of writing their own short story using **-ve** words. Explain to the children that using the words in this way will help them to remember the words more effectively. Encourage the children to include as many of the Word Bank words as possible.
2. Use the following text as a model to show how to write the story, or alternatively, use the text as passage dictation by reading each sentence slowly and clearly for the children to write down:

The **detective** put on his **gloves** and left the train. He saw a white **dove** sitting on top of the big clock. It was **twelve** o'clock. He was going to **have olives** with his lunch. I **love olives** he thought.

Think about it!

1. Ask the children to read the words in the Think about it! box. Ask them to think carefully and talk with a partner about the vowel sound.
2. Ask the children what vowel sound they can hear in the words. Elicit ideas and establish that the letter **o** is representing an /u/ sound in these words.
3. Tell children that they need to be aware of these words so that they don't accidentally spell them with a letter **u** rather than a letter **o**.

Optional: Review the Letterland character stories

You might want to introduce the story of Oscar's Bothersome Brother.

Review previous learning

Ask the children if they can recall the spelling rule or any example words from the previous spelling lesson. Elicit ideas and remind the children that: The sound /v/ is usually spelt as **ve** if it comes at the end of a word, for example: ha**ve**, gi**ve**.

OBJECTIVES
PART 2 -**tch**
Spell and use words in writing containing -**tch**

Introducing the rule

Explain to the children that in today's lesson they will learn about words that are spelt with **tch**.

The /ch/ sound is usually spelt as -**tch** if it comes straight after a single vowel letter (short vowel sounds), for example: ma**tch**, sti**tch**, fe**tch**.

Optional: Review the Letterland character stories

Character-based stories can help children to remember spelling patterns (see page 120).

Pupil Book Activity 1: Picture Match

1. Draw children' attention to the Word Bank at the top of page 7. Explain that all of the words include the /ch/ sound but these words all end in the spelling pattern -**tch**.
2. Ask the children to read through the words in the Word Bank and talk to a partner about what they mean. Then ask the children if there are any words they are unsure of and explain the meanings to them, looking in the dictionary for a definition if necessary.
3. Ask the children to find and copy words from the Word Bank to match the pictures.

Answers: a) watch; b) hutch; c) kitchen; d) match; e) catch

Pupil Book Activity 2: Underline tch

1. Model the activity by choosing a word from the Word Bank and writing it on the board, for example: **watch**. Then underline the **tch** part of the word: wa**tch**.
2. Ask children to underline the **tch** spelling pattern in all of the words in the Word Bank. Ask: Does the **tch** pattern always come at the end of the words? (No, see **kitchen** and **ketchup**).

Pupil Book Activity 3: Circle the Vowel

1. Ask children to tell you what the vowel letters are (**a**, **e**, **i**, **o**, **u**). Remind the children of the spelling rule – that a word is usually spelt with **tch** if it comes after single vowel letter.

2. Ask the children to go back through the words in the Word Bank and this time use a coloured pen or pencil to circle the vowel letter that comes before the **tch** pattern. Ask children to read the words and listen carefully to check if the vowel letter represents a short vowel sound.

Pupil Book Activity 4: Complete the Sentences

1. Read sentences **a – e** to the children pausing as you reach each gap. Complete the first sentence with the children by re-reading to the first gap and then say: Look at the Word Bank. Which word is something you could eat with chips? Elicit children' ideas and establish that the word is **ketchup**.
2. Ask children to fill the gaps in the rest of the sentences independently or with a partner.

Answers: a) ketchup; b) hutch; c) match; d) catch; e) kitchen

Pupil Book Activity 5: Challenge!

1. Draw the children's attention to the Word Search at the bottom of page 7. Set children the challenge of finding five **ve** and five **tch** words in the Word Search. Eight of the words run horizontally from left to right and two words run vertically from top to bottom.
2. Tell the children to circle each word as they find it and then write the words in the box.

g	i	v	e	g	r	y	l
a	h	a	v	e	w	s	i
o	b	p	d	o	v	e	v
p	l	o	v	e	c	h	e
a	t	i	l	a	t	c	h
t	u	m	a	t	c	h	d
c	f	k	h	u	t	c	h
h	s	t	i	t	c	h	l

-ve	-tch
give	patch
have	latch
live	match
dove	hutch
love	stitch

Assessment: -ve, tch

Tell the children that you will say the word, and then you will read out a sentence containing the word to help them know what it means. You will then repeat the word on its own before pausing so that the children can write the word down. For example: 1. **have**. I have a new book. **have**

1. **have**. I **have** a new book. **have**
2. **catch**. We like to play **catch**. **catch**
3. **give**. I will **give** the ball to Peter. **give**
4. **itch**. My cat has an **itch**. **itch**
5. **live**. We **live** in a small village. **live**
6. **match**. I played in a football **match**. **match**
7. **olive**. We have an **olive** tree in the garden. **olive**
8. **fetch**. The dog will **fetch** the stick. **fetch**
9. **love**. I **love** my soft bed. **love**
10. **hutch**. Our rabbit lives in a **hutch**. **hutch**

For those students who need a bit more of a spelling challenge, read out the five further 'Quiet Zone' words to spell: **glove**, **active**, **kitchen**, **switch**, **stretch**.

STATION - WEEK 4
Foxes Family

OBJECTIVES
PART 1 –s, –es
Spell and use words in writing ending in –s and –es

Review previous learning

Ask the children if they can recall the spelling rule or any example words from the previous spelling lesson. Elicit ideas and remind the children that: The /ch/ sound is usually spelt as **tch** if it comes straight after a single vowel letter (short vowel sounds), for example: **match**, **stitch**, **fetch**.

Introducing the rule

Explain to the children that in today's lesson they will learn about words that are spelt with –**s** and words that are spelt with –**es**.

If the ending sounds like /s/ or /z/, it is spelt as –**s**, for example, cat**s**. If the ending sounds like /e+z/ and forms an extra syllable or 'beat' in the word, it is spelt as –**es**, for example, box**es**.

Optional: Review the Letterland character stories
Letterland stories help children to remember these sounds. (see page 121).

Optional: Review the Letterland Grammar analogies
Learn the analogy to help children understand plural noun suffixes (see page 127).

Pupil Book Activity 1: Picture Match

1. Draw children's attention to the Word Bank at the top of page 8. Explain that all of these words contain either –**s** or –**es**.
2. Ask the children to read through the words in the Word Bank and talk to a partner about what they mean. Then ask the children if there are any words they are unsure of and explain the meanings to them, looking in the dictionary for a definition if necessary.
3. Ask the children to find and copy words from the Word Bank to match the pictures.

Answers: a) foxes; b) pens; c) dogs; d) brushes; e) cats; f) buses

Pupil Book Activity 2: Underline –s and –es

1. Model the activity by choosing a word from the Word Bank and writing it on the board, for example: **dogs**. Then underline the –**s** (or –**es**) part of the word: **dogs**.
2. Ask the children to underline the –**s** and –**es** spelling pattern in all of the words in the Word Bank. Ask: Does the –**s** and –**es** pattern always come at the end of the words? (Yes, in this case they are suffixes – endings of words)

Pupil Book Activity 3: Circle the Vowel

1. Ask children to tell you what the vowel letters are (**a**, **e**, **i**, **o**, **u**).
2. Ask the children to go back through the words in the Word Bank and this time use a coloured pen or pencil to circle the vowel letter that comes before the –**s** (or –**es**) suffix. Ask children to read the words and listen carefully to check if the vowel letter represents a short vowel sound.

Pupil Book Activity 4: Complete the Sentences

1. Read sentences **a – e** to the children, pausing as you reach each gap. Complete the first sentence with the children by re-reading to the first gap and then say: Look at the Word Bank. Which animals like to play 'fetch'? Elicit children's ideas and establish that the word is **dogs**.
2. Ask the children to fill in the gaps in the rest of the sentences independently or with a partner.

Answers: a) dogs; b) hats; c) buses; d) brushes; e) pens

Pupil Book Activity 5: Challenge!

1. Set the children the challenge of writing their own short story using **-s** and **-es** words. Explain to the children that using the words in this way will help them to remember the words more effectively. Encourage the children to include as many of the Word Bank words as possible.
2. Use the following text as a model to show the children how to write the short story or, alternatively, use the text as a passage dictation by reading each sentence slowly and clearly for the children to write down:

When I got home from school I walked my **dogs**. Then I got the paint **brushes** out to do some painting. I painted a picture of three **buses**. I found my **pens** and wrote my name on the picture. Then I saw my **cats** hiding in some **hats**.

Additional teaching notes

1. To show that there is more than one item we can usually use the ending **-s**. An ending like this is called a suffix.
2. We use **-es** at the end of some words to show more than one item. We use **-es** if the word for the single item ends in the letters **ch**, **sh**, **s**, **x** or **z**.

Review previous learning

Ask the children if they can recall the spelling rule or any example words from the previous spelling lesson. Elicit ideas and remind the children that: If the ending sounds like /s/ or /z/, it is spelt as **-s**, for example, cat**s**. If the ending sounds like /e+z/ and forms an extra syllable or 'beat' in the word, it is spelt as **-es**, for example, box**es**.

> **OBJECTIVES**
> **PART 2 – y**
> Spell and use words in writing ending in **-y**

Introducing the rule

Explain to the children that in today's lesson they will learn about words that are spelt with **-y**.

The sound /ee/ is usually spelt as **-y** if it comes at the end of the word, for example: **happy**, **funny**.

> **Optional:** Review the Letterland character stories
> Character-based stories can help children to remember spelling patterns (see page 121).

Pupil Book Activity 1: Picture Match

1. Draw the children's attention to the Word Bank at the top of page 9. Explain that all of these words end in **-y**.
2. Ask the children to read through the words in the Word Bank and talk to a partner about what they mean. Then ask the children if there are any words they are unsure of and explain the meanings to them, looking in the dictionary for a definition if necessary.
3. Ask the children to find and copy words from the Word Bank to match the pictures.

Answers: a) muddy; b) carry; c) rainy

Pupil Book Activity 2: Word Match

1. Draw the children's attention to the words written underneath the blank drawing boxes.
2. Ask the children to read each word and talk to a partner about what they mean.
3. Ask the children to draw a simple picture to match the words underneath each box, for example, to match the word 'family', children could draw their family.

Pupil Book Activity 3: Complete the Sentences

1. Read sentences **a** – **e** to the children, pausing as you reach each gap. Complete the first sentence with the children by re-reading to the first gap and then say: Look at the Word Bank. Which word is something that the weather might be if it is hot? Elicit the children's ideas and establish that the word is **sunny**.
2. Ask the children to fill in the gaps in the rest of the sentences independently or with a partner.

Answers: a) sunny; b) grumpy; c) muddy; d) silly; e) carry

Pupil Book Activity 4: Challenge!

1. Draw the children's attention to the Word Search at the bottom of page 9. Set children the challenge of finding ten –**y** words in the Word Search. Eight of the words run horizontally from left to right and two words run vertically from top to bottom.
2. Tell the children to circle each word as they find it and then write the words in the correct column.

Answers:

h	a	p	p	y	d	k	e
f	c	p	a	r	t	y	l
u	m	u	d	d	y	j	f
n	g	c	a	r	r	y	a
n	s	i	l	l	y	h	m
y	g	r	u	m	p	y	i
b	f	r	a	i	n	y	l
s	u	n	n	y	a	i	y

-y	
happy	carry
funny	silly
party	grumpy
muddy	rainy
family	sunny

Watch Out!

1. Ask the children to read the words in the Watch Out! box: **monkey**, **donkey**.
2. Explain that some words that end in an /ee/ sound end in the letters –**ey** instead of just –**y**.

Assessment: -s, -es, -y

Tell the children that you are going to read out ten words, one at a time. Each word will be one of the –**s**, -**es** or –**y** words that they have been learning. Tell the children that you will say the word, and then you will read out a sentence containing the word to help them know what it means. You will then repeat the word on its own before pausing so that the children can write the word down. For example: 1. **cats**. My **cats** like to sleep all day. **cats**

1. **cats**. My **cats** like to sleep all day. **cats**
2. **happy**. Playing with my friends makes me feel **happy**. **happy**
3. **pens**. I have a pot of **pens** on my desk. **pens**

4. **muddy**. My dog loves to get wet and **muddy**. **muddy**
5. **hats**. My dad wears lots of **hats**. **hats**
6. **sunny**. Today is a **sunny** day. **sunny**
7. **foxes**. Dad says that **foxes** have been in our garden. **foxes**
8. **family**. There are lots of people in my **family**. **family**
9. **buses**. We saw lots of **buses** on our journey. **buses**
10. **grumpy**. I felt **grumpy** when I got up early. **grumpy**

For those students who need a bit more of a spelling challenge, read out the five further 'Quiet Zone' words to spell: **chats**, **watches**, **funny**, **silly**, **dirty**.

Full details of how to carry out assessment can be found on pages 6 and 108 of this guide.

Spelling Games

Remember there are activities and games provided at the back of this guide. These are optional and can be used at an time to consolidate learning. Each game is 'train themed' so your class can really embrace the idea of Spelling Stations!

STATION - WEEK 5
Pink Picnic

OBJECTIVES
PART 1 – nk
Spell and use words in writing containing **nk**

Review previous learning

Ask the children if they can recall the spelling rule or any example words from the previous spelling lesson. Elicit ideas and remind the children that: The sound /ee/ is usually spelt as –**y** if it comes at the end of the word, for example: **happy**, **funny**.

Introducing the rule

Explain to the children that in today's lesson they will learn about words that are spelt with **nk**.

The sound /ng/ is spelt **n** before **k**, for example: **bank**, **pink**.

> **Optional:** **Review the Letterland character stories**
> Character-based stories can help children to remember spelling patterns (see page 121).

Pupil Book Activity 1: Picture Match

1. Draw children's attention to the Word Bank at the top of page 10. Explain that all of these words contain **nk**.
2. Ask the children to read through the words in the Word Bank and talk to a partner about what they mean. Then ask the children if there are any words they are unsure of and explain the meanings to them, looking in the dictionary for a definition if necessary.
3. Ask the children to find and copy words from the Word Bank to match the pictures.

Answers: a) bank; b) sink; c) pink; d) wink; e) drink; f) think

Pupil Book Activity 2: Underline nk

1. Model the activity by choosing a word from the Word Bank and writing it on the board, for example: **bank**. Then underline the **nk** part of the word: **ba**<u>**nk**</u>.
2. Ask the children to underline the **nk** spelling pattern in all of the words in the Word Bank. Ask: *Does the **nk** pattern always come at the end of the words? (Yes, unless the word has a suffix or is a compound word)*

Pupil Book Activity 3: Complete the Sentences

1. Read sentences **a – e** to the children, pausing as you reach each gap. Complete the first sentence with the children by re-reading to the first gap and then say: *Look at the Word Bank. Which word is something you might say after you are given a gift?* Elicit children's ideas and establish that the word is **thank** [you].
2. Ask the children to fill in the gaps in the rest of the sentences independently or with a partner.

Answers: a) thank; b) pink; c) sank; d) drink; e) bank

Pupil Book Activity 4: Challenge!

1. Set the children the challenge of writing their own short story using **nk** words. Explain to the children that using the words in this way will help them to remember the words more effectively. Encourage the children to include as many of the Word Bank words as possible.

2. Use the following text as a model to show the children how to write the short story or, alternatively, use the text as a passage dictation by reading each sentence slowly and clearly for the children to write down:

Mark put his pocket money into the **bank**. He said, "I **think** it will be safe there." After he said **thank** you to the cashier for her help he went to the farm. At the farm he saw geese who went, "**honk, honk**!" His **pink** welly boots **sank** into the mud. "Those geese **stink**!" he said. After a long day he had a big **drink** of water.

> **OBJECTIVES**
> **PART 2 – Syllables**
> Spell and use words in writing containing more than one syllable

Review previous learning

Ask the children if they can recall the spelling rule or any example words from the previous spelling lesson. Elicit ideas and remind the children that: The sound /ng/ is spelt **n** before **k**, for example: **bank**, **pink**.

Introducing the rule

Explain to the children that in today's lesson they will learn about words that contain more than one syllable. Each syllable is like a 'beat' in the word. Words of more than one syllable often have a vowel sound that is unclear.

Pupil Book Activity 1: Picture Match

1. Draw the children's attention to the Word Bank at the top of page 11. Explain that all of these words contain more than one syllable.
2. Ask the children to read through the words in the Word Bank and talk to a partner about what they mean. Then ask the children if there are any words they are unsure of and explain the meanings to them, looking in the dictionary for a definition if necessary.
3. Ask the children to read the words in unison with you and to clap each beat. Ask how many syllables there are in each word (they all have two). Explain that when words have more than one syllable we can break the words down to think about how to spell each syllable through the word in turn. Remind the children that often one of the syllables contains an unstressed vowel that may be difficult to identify and therefore needs to be learnt.
4. Ask the children to find and copy words from the Word Bank to match the pictures.

Answers: a) rabbit; b) robot; c) robin

Pupil Book Activity 2: Word Match

1. Draw the children's attention to the words written underneath the blank drawing boxes.
2. Ask the children to read each word and talk to a partner about what they mean.
3. Ask the children to draw a simple picture to match the words underneath each box, for example, to match the word 'carrot', children could draw a carrot, or a rabbit eating a carrot.

Pupil Book Activity 3: Complete the Sentences

1. Read sentences **a – e** to the children, pausing as you reach each gap. Complete the first sentence with the children by re-reading to the first gap and then say: Look at the Word Bank. Which word is somewhere that you might keep a coin? Elicit the children's ideas and establish that the word is **pocket**.
2. Ask the children to fill in the gaps in the rest of the sentences independently or with a partner.

Answers: a) pocket; b) tractor; c) rabbit; d) thunder; e) robin

Pupil Book Activity 4: Challenge!

1. Draw the children's attention to the Word Search at the bottom of page 11. Set children the challenge of finding ten two-syllable words in the Word Search. Eight of the words run horizontally from left to right and two words run vertically from top to bottom.
2. Tell the children to circle each word as they find it and then write the words in the box.
   Answers:

t	h	u	n	d	e	r	r
r	p	o	c	k	e	t	o
a	b	r	o	b	o	t	b
b	p	i	c	n	i	c	i
b	c	a	r	r	o	t	n
i	d	r	a	g	o	n	r
t	a	m	u	f	f	i	n
t	r	a	c	t	o	r	c

two syllables	
thunder	robin
picnic	carrot
rabbit	dragon
pocket	robot
muffin	tractor

Think about it!

1. Ask the children to read the words in the Think about it! box: **butterfly**, **elephant**, **computer**.
2. Ask them to read each word aloud and clap the beats to count how many syllables there are. (There are three syllables in these words)

Assessment: nk, syllables

Tell the children that you are going to read out ten words, one at a time. Each word will be one of the **ng** or two-syllable words that they have been learning. Tell the children that you will say the word, and then you will read out a sentence containing the word to help them know what it means. You will then repeat the word on its own before pausing so that the children can write the word down. For example: 1. **bank**. I put the money in the **bank**. bank

1. **bank**. I put the money in the **bank**. **bank**
2. **rabbit**. We have a pet **rabbit**. **rabbit**
3. **think**. I **think** I would like to read a book. **think**
4. **carrot**. Our rabbit is eating a **carrot**. **carrot**
5. **sank**. My foot **sank** into the mud. **sank**
6. **pocket**. I have lots of things in my **pocket**. **pocket**
7. **pink**. The flowers are **pink**. **pink**
8. **sunset**. We watched the **sunset**. **sunset**
9. **honk**. The horn went '**honk**'! **honk**
10. **picnic**. I love to go on a **picnic**. **picnic**

For those students who need a bit more of a spelling challenge, read out the five further 'Quiet Zone' words to spell: **drink**, **thank**, **thunder**, **robin**, **salad**.

Full details of how to carry out assessment can be found on pages 6 and 108 of this guide.

STATION - WEEK 6
Kick**ing** Play**er**

OBJECTIVES
PART 1 –**ing**
Spell and use verbs in writing ending in -ing

Review previous learning

Ask the children if they can recall the spelling rule or any example words from the previous spelling lesson. Elicit ideas and remind the children that: Each syllable is like a 'beat' in the word. Words of more than one syllable often have a vowel sound that is unclear.

Introducing the rule

Explain to the children that in today's lesson they will learn about words that are spelt with –**ing** at the end. The ending –**ing** always adds an extra syllable to the word. If the verb ends in two consonant letters (the same or different), the ending is simply added on, for example, **hunting**, **buzzing**.

> **Optional: Review the Letterland character stories**
> Character-based stories can help children to remember spelling patterns (see page 121).

> **Optional: Review the Letterland Grammar analogies**
> Learn the analogy to help children understand suffixes added to verbs (see page 127).

Pupil Book Activity 1: Picture Match

1. Draw children's attention to the Word Bank at the top of page 12. Explain that all of these words end in the –**ing** spelling pattern.
2. Ask the children to read through the words in the Word Bank and talk to a partner about what they mean. Then ask the children if there are any words they are unsure of and explain the meanings to them, looking in the dictionary for a definition if necessary.
3. Ask the children to find and copy words from the Word Bank to match the pictures.

Answers: a) singing; b) telling; c) banging; d) kicking; e) adding; f) spending

Pupil Book Activity 2: Underline ing

1. Model the activity by choosing a word from the Word Bank and writing it on the board, for example: **singing**. Then underline the **ing** part of the word: sing**ing**.
1. Ask the children to underline the **ing** spelling pattern in all of the words in the Word Bank.

Pupil Book Activity 3: Circle the consonant letters

1. Ask the children to tell you what the consonant letters are (**b**, **c**, **d**, **f**, **g**, **h**, **j**, **k**, **l**, **m**, **n**, **p**, **q**, **r**, **s**, **t**, **v**, **w**, **x**, **y**, **z**). Remind the children of the spelling rule – that if the word ends in two consonant letters the -**ing** ending is simply added on.
2. Ask the children to go back through the words in the Word Bank and this time use a coloured pen or pencil to circle the consonant letters that come before the –**ing** patterns. Ask the children if all of the words have two consonant letters before the –**ing** pattern. (No, they do not, for example, eat**ing**, sail**ing**).

Pupil Book Activity 4: Complete the Sentences

1. Read sentences **a – e** to the children, pausing as you reach each gap. Complete the first sentence with the children by re-reading to the first gap and then say: Look at the Word Bank. Which word is something you might do to a drum? Elicit children's ideas and establish that the word is **banging**.
2. Ask the children to fill in the gaps in the rest of the sentences independently or with a partner.

Answers: a) banging; b) telling; c) hunting; d) singing; e) jumping

Pupil Book Activity 5: Challenge!

1. Set the children the challenge of writing their own short story using **-ing** words. Explain to the children that using the words in this way will help them to remember the words more effectively. Encourage the children to include as many of the Word Bank words as possible.
2. Use the following text as a model to show the children how to write the short story or, alternatively, use the text as a passage dictation by reading each sentence slowly and clearly for the children to write down:

Nisha and Sid were **singing** as they went to the park. Their dog, Harvey, was **jumping** up. At the park they saw some children **spending** pocket money getting ice creams. There were carefully **adding** up the coins. Sid looked at Nisha. She was **hunting** in her bag to see if they had some coins to spend too.

Watch Out!

1. Draw the children's attention to the Watch Out! box at the bottom of the page.
2. Explain to the children that after a short vowel sound the rule is to double the final letter and then add **-ing**.
3. Write the examples on the board, **shop – shopping** and **run – running**, and draw children's attention to the short vowel sounds and doubled consonant letters.

> **Optional: Review the Letterland character stories**
> The 'Best Friends to the Rescue' story is a useful reminder to children about doubling consonants.

Additional teaching notes

To extend knowledge further you could introduce the rule that words ending in an **e**, drop the **e** before adding **-ing**. For example, **bake – baking**, **make – making**, **hope – hoping**.

OBJECTIVES
PART 2 -er + verbs
Spell and use verbs in writing ending in -er

Review previous learning

Ask the children if they can recall the spelling rule or any example words from the previous spelling lesson. Elicit ideas and remind the children that: The ending **-ing** always adds an extra syllable to the word. If the verb ends in two consonant letters (the same or different), the ending is simply added on, for example, **hunting**, **buzzing**.

Introducing the rule

Explain to the children that in today's lesson they will learn about words that are spelt with **-er** at the end. The ending **-er** always adds an extra syllable to the word. If the verb ends in two consonant letters (the same or different), the ending is simply added on, for example, **hunter**, **buzzer**.

Optional: Review the Letterland character stories
Character-based stories can help children to remember spelling patterns (see page 121).

Pupil Book Activity 1: Picture Match

1. Draw the children's attention to the Word Bank at the top of page 13. Explain that all of these words end in –**er**.
2. Ask the children to read through the words in the Word Bank and talk to a partner about what they mean. Then ask the children if there are any words they are unsure of and explain the meanings to them, looking in the dictionary for a definition if necessary.
3. Ask the children to find and copy words from the Word Bank to match the pictures.

Answers: a) painter; b) farmer; c) singer

Pupil Book Activity 2: Word Match

1. Draw the children's attention to the words written underneath the blank drawing boxes.
2. Ask the children to read each word and talk to a partner about what they mean.
3. Ask the children to draw a simple picture to match the words underneath each box, for example, to match the word 'teacher', children could draw a picture of you.

Pupil Book Activity 3: Complete the Sentences

1. Read sentences **a – e** to the children, pausing as you reach each gap. Complete the first sentence with the children by re-reading to the first gap and then say: Look at the word in the Word Bank. Elicit the children's ideas and establish that the word is **gardener**.
2. Ask the children to fill in the gaps in the rest of the sentences independently or with a partner.

Answers: a) gardener; b) banker; c) singer; d) player; e) cleaner

Pupil Book Activity 4: Challenge!

1. Draw the children's attention to the Word Search at the bottom of page 13. Set children the challenge of finding ten –**ing** and –**er** words in the Word Search. Nine of the words run horizontally from left to right and one word runs vertically from top to bottom.
2. Tell the children to circle each word as they find it and then write the words in the correct column.

Answers:

p	a	i	n	t	e	r	c	p
b	a	n	k	e	r	p	t	u
g	b	a	r	k	i	n	g	l
c	s	i	n	g	e	r	s	l
s	a	i	l	i	n	g	d	i
r	u	s	h	i	n	g	o	n
f	a	r	m	e	r	k	p	g
s	m	o	a	n	i	n	g	l
t	h	e	l	p	e	r	a	s

-ing	-er
pulling	painter
barking	banker
sailing	singer
rushing	farmer
moaning	helper

32

Watch Out!

1. Draw the children's attention to the Watch Out! box at the bottom of the page.
2. Explain to the children that after a short vowel sound the rule is to double the final letter, then add **–er**.
3. Write the examples on the board, **dig – digger** and **run – runner** and draw children's attention to the short vowel sounds and doubled consonant letters.

Additional teaching notes

To extend knowledge further you could introduce the rule that words ending in an **e**, drop the **e** before adding –er. For example, **bake – baker**.

Assessment: -ing, -er

Tell the children that you are going to read out ten words, one at a time. Each word will be one of the –**ing** or –**er** words that they have been learning. Tell the children that you will say the word, and then you will read out a sentence containing the word to help them know what it means. You will then repeat the word on its own before pausing so that the children can write the word down. For example: 1. **jumping**. I love **jumping** on the trampoline. **jumping**

1. **jumping**. I love **jumping** on the trampoline. **jumping**
2. **player**. The football **player** wore orange socks. **player**
3. **singing**. You can hear me **singing** in the shower. **singing**
4. **helper**. We have a **helper** in our class. **helper**
5. **banging**. I love **banging** the drums. **banging**
6. **farmer**. The **farmer** milked the cows. **farmer**
7. **sailing**. I would like to go **sailing** on a boat. **sailing**
8. **kicking**. I am good at **kicking** the ball. **kicking**
9. **painter**. Picasso was a famous **painter**. **painter**
10. **gardener**. The **gardener** mowed the lawn. **gardener**

For those students who need a bit more of a spelling challenge, read out the five further 'Quiet Zone' words to spell: **spending, telling, hunting, singing, banker**.

Full details of how to carry out assessment can be found on pages 6 and 108 of this guide.

STATION - WEEK 7
Stopped Longer

OBJECTIVES
PART 1 –ed + verbs
Spell and use verbs in writing ending in -ed

Review previous learning

Ask the children if they can recall the spelling rule or any example words from the previous spelling lesson. Elicit ideas and remind the children that: The ending –**er** always adds an extra syllable to the word. If the verb ends in two consonant letters (the same or different), the ending is simply added on, for example, **hunter**, **buzzer**.

Introducing the rule

Explain to the children that in today's lesson they will learn about words that are spelt with –**ed** at the end. The ending –**ed** sometimes adds an extra syllable to the word. If the verb ends in two consonant letters (the same or different), the ending is simply added on, for example, **hunted**, **buzzed**.

Optional: Review the Letterland character stories

The Letterland stories and the three sounds of the –**ed** suffix (page 121).

Optional: Review the Letterland Grammar analogies

Learn the analogy to help children understand suffixes added to verbs (see page 127).

Pupil Book Activity 1: Picture Match

1. Draw children's attention to the Word Bank at the top of page 14. Explain that all of these words end in the –**ed** spelling pattern.
2. Ask the children to read through the words in the Word Bank and talk to a partner about what they mean. Then ask the children if there are any words they are unsure of and explain the meanings to them, looking in the dictionary for a definition if necessary. Ask the children to talk about the sound represented by the –**ed** letters. Ask: is it always an /e+d/ sound? (No, see lock**ed**, watch**ed**, park**ed**, talk**ed**, help**ed**)
3. Ask the children to find and copy words from the Word Bank to match the pictures.

Answers: a) melted; b) locked; c) lifted; d) watched; e) parked; f) talked

Pupil Book Activity 2: Underline ed

1. Model the activity by choosing a word from the Word Bank and writing it on the board, for example: **parked**. Then underline the **ed** part of the word: **park<u>ed</u>**.
2. Ask the children to underline the **ed** spelling pattern in all of the words in the Word Bank.

Pupil Book Activity 3: Circle the consonant letters

1. Ask the children to tell you what the consonant letters are (**b, c, d, f, g, h, j, k, l, m, n, p, q, r, s, t, v, w, x, y, z**). Remind the children of the spelling rule – that if the word ends in two consonant letters the –**ed** ending is simply added on.
2. Ask the children to go back through the words in the Word Bank and this time use a coloured pen or pencil to circle the consonant letters that come before the –**ed** patterns. Ask the children if all of the words have two consonant letters before the –**ed** pattern. (No, they do not, for example, **opened**).

Pupil Book Activity 4: Complete the Sentences

1. Read sentences **a** – **e** to the children, pausing as you reach each gap. Complete the first sentence with the children by re-reading to the first gap and then say: Look at the words in the Word Bank. Elicit children's ideas and establish that the word is **watched**.
2. Ask the children to fill in the gaps in the rest of the sentences independently or with a partner.

Answers: a) watched; b) melted; c) talked; d) sorted; e) parked

Pupil Book Activity 5: Challenge!

1. Set the children the challenge of writing their own short story using –**ed** words. Explain to the children that using the words in this way will help them to remember the words more effectively. Encourage the children to include as many of the Word Bank words as possible.
2. Use the following text as a model to show the children how to write the short story or, alternatively, use the text as a passage dictation by reading each sentence slowly and clearly for the children to write down:

Mum **parked** our car next to the shop. Freya's ice cream had **melted** and Mum wanted to buy some wet wipes. I sat in the car and **watched** people walking by. I talked to Freya. She tried to open the car door but it was still **locked**. Mum **opened** it and **helped** her get **sorted** out. What a mess!

Did you know?

1. Draw the children's attention to the Did you know? box at the bottom of the page.
2. Explain to the children that the past tense of some verbs may sound as if they end in /e+d/ (an extra syllable), some sound like /d/ or /t/ but they are all spelt with –**ed**. This can make spelling these words tricky.
3. Model on the board how you might sound out and spell the word **parked**. It sounds like it will end in a 't'.
4. Ask the children to re-read the words in the Word Bank and tell you the end sounds. Remember, if children struggle with remembering the three sounds of –**ed**, the Letterland character stories may help fix the idea in their minds.

Review previous learning

Ask the children if they can recall the spelling rule or any example words from the previous spelling lesson. Elicit ideas and remind the children that: The ending –**ed** sometimes adds an extra syllable to the word. If the verb ends in two consonant letters (the same or different), the ending is simply added on, for example, **hunted**, **buzzed**.

> **OBJECTIVES**
> **PART 2** –**er** + adjectives
> Spell and use adjectives in writing ending in –**er**

Introducing the rule

Explain to the children that in today's lesson they will learn about words that are spelt with –**er**.

The ending –**er** always adds an extra syllable to the word. If the word ends in two consonant letters (the same or different), the ending is simply added on, for example, **grander**, **fresher**.

Optional: Review the Letterland character stories

Character-based stories can help children to remember spelling patterns (page 121).

Optional: Review the Letterland Grammar analogies

Use the analogy to explain how suffixes can be added to form adjectives (see page 127).

Pupil Book Activity 1: Picture Match

1. Draw the children's attention to the Word Bank at the top of page 15. Explain that all of these words end in –**er**.
2. Ask the children to read through the words in the Word Bank and talk to a partner about what they mean. Then ask the children if there are any words they are unsure of and explain the meanings to them, looking in the dictionary for a definition if necessary.
3. Ask the children to find and copy words from the Word Bank to match the pictures.

Answers: a) higher; b) colder; c) younger

Pupil Book Activity 2: Word Match

1. Draw the children's attention to the words written underneath the blank drawing boxes.
2. Ask the children to read each word and talk to a partner about what they mean.
3. Ask the children to draw a simple picture to match the words underneath each box; for example, to match the word 'taller', children could draw two children, one of whom is taller.

Pupil Book Activity 3: Complete the Sentences

1. Read sentences **a – e** to the children, pausing as you reach each gap. Complete the first sentence with the children by re-reading to the first gap and then say: Look at the words in the Word Bank. Elicit the children's ideas for the word which works best in the gap. Establish that the word is **taller**.
2. Ask the children to fill in the gaps in the rest of the sentences independently or with a partner.

Answers: a) taller; b) quicker; c) colder; d) older; e) higher

Pupil Book Activity 4: Challenge!

1. Draw the children's attention to the Word Search at the bottom of page 15. Set children the challenge of finding ten –**ed** and –**er** words in the Word Search. Eight of the words run horizontally from left to right and two words run vertically from top to bottom.
2. Tell the children to circle each word as they find it and then write the words in the correct column.

Answers:

h	s	h	o	r	t	e	r
i	w	a	t	c	h	e	d
g	m	e	l	t	e	d	t
h	l	h	e	l	p	e	d
e	o	c	o	l	d	e	r
r	w	s	o	r	t	e	d
c	e	w	a	r	m	e	r
a	r	p	a	r	k	e	d

-ed	-er
watched	higher
melted	shorter
helped	lower
sorted	colder
parked	warmer

Watch Out!

1. Draw children's attention to the Watch Out! box.
2. Explain that when we add –**er** to words ending in **e**, we drop the **e**. For example, **brave** – **braver**, **wise** – **wiser**.

Assessment: -ed, -er

Tell the children that you are going to read out ten words, one at a time. Each word will be one of the **–ed** or **–er** words that they have been learning. Tell the children that you will say the word, and then you will read out a sentence containing the word to help them know what it means. You will then repeat the word on its own before pausing so that the children can write the word down. For example: **1. melted**. The ice cube melted. **melted**

1. **melted**. The ice cube **melted**. **melted**
2. **lifted**. I **lifted** the box onto the shelf. **lifted**
3. **rested**. After school I **rested**. **rested**
4. **locked**. Mum **locked** the door. **locked**
5. **sorted**. I **sorted** the mixed up puzzles. **sorted**
6. **shorter**. I am **shorter** than Isabel. **shorter**
7. **lower**. I put my book on the **lower** shelf. **lower**
8. **quicker**. Ali can type **quicker** than me. **quicker**
9. **slower**. I am **slower** at reading than Liam. **slower**
10. **colder**. The weather is getting **colder**. **colder**

For those students who need a bit more of a spelling challenge, read out the five further 'Quiet Zone' words to spell: **talked**, **watched**, **opened**, **taller**, **warmer**.

Full details of how to carry out assessment can be found on pages 6 and 108 of this guide.

STATION - WEEK 8

The Quickest

**OBJECTIVES
PART 1 – Tricky Words**

Spell and use some common exception tricky words in writing

Review previous learning

Ask the children if they can recall the spelling rule or any example words from the previous spelling lesson. Elicit ideas and remind the children that: The ending –**er** always adds an extra syllable to the word. If the verb ends in two consonant letters (the same or different), the ending is simply added on, for example, **grander**, **fresher**.

Introducing the rule

Explain to the children that in today's lesson they will learn about words that can be difficult to spell because the letter-sound correspondences in them have not yet been taught, but the words are so useful that we want to use them now.

Some words do not sound the way you might expect them to. Pay attention to which parts of the word you know and which parts are tricky.

Pupil Book Activity 1: Read the Word Bank and Example Sentences

1. Draw the children's attention to the Word Bank in the left-hand column of page 16. Explain that all of these words contain parts that have not yet been taught but that it is likely the children will know how to read the words from encountering them in reading books.
2. Ask the children to read through the words in the Word Bank and talk to a partner about what they mean. Then ask the children if there are any words they are unsure of and explain the meanings to them, looking in the dictionary for a definition if necessary.
3. Ask the children to read the example sentences in the second column to help them understand the words in context.

Pupil Book Activity 2: Colour the Parts

1. Draw the children's attention to the third column which contains the words shown so that each phoneme (sound) is distinguishable.
2. Ask the children to say the sounds while thinking carefully about the whole word. Remind them that the letters may not sound the way they expect.
3. Ask the children to colour the easy parts of the words in green and the tricky parts in orange. For example in the word 'the' the 'th' letters represent the /th/ sound but the 'e' letter represents an /uh/ sound. Alternatively ask them to write a wiggly line under the tricky part.

Pupil Book Activity 3: Write the Word

1. In the final column ask the children to write each word. If they feel confident they could cover up the information in the other columns. If they lack confidence they should copy the spelling from the other columns and say the word as they write it.
2. Remind the children to look back through their spellings to check for accuracy.

Review previous learning

Ask the children if they can recall the spelling rule or any example words from the previous spelling lesson. Elicit ideas and remind the children that: Some words do not sound the way you might expect them to, for example, **said**, **says**, **were**. Pay attention to which parts of the word you know and which parts are tricky.

OBJECTIVES
PART 2 –est
Spell and use adjectives in writing ending in -est

Introducing the rule

Explain to the children that in today's lesson they will learn about words that are spelt with **-est** at the end. The ending **-est** always adds an extra syllable to the word. If the adjective ends in two consonant letters (the same or different), the ending is simply added on, for example, **quickest**, **smartest**.

Optional: Review the Letterland character stories
Character-based stories can help children to remember spelling patterns (see page 121).

Optional: Review the Letterland Grammar analogies
Use the analogy to explain how suffixes can be added to form adjectives (see page 127).

Pupil Book Activity 1: Picture Match

1. Draw children's attention to the Word Bank at the top of page 17. Explain that all of these words end in the **-est** spelling pattern.
2. Ask the children to read through the words in the Word Bank and talk to a partner about what they mean. Then ask the children if there are any words they are unsure of and explain the meanings to them, looking in the dictionary for a definition if necessary.
3. Ask the children to find and copy words from the Word Bank to match the pictures.

Answers: a) tallest; b) strongest; c) freshest; d) fastest; e) grandest; f) youngest

Pupil Book Activity 2: Underline est

1. Model the activity by choosing a word from the Word Bank and writing it on the board, for example: **strongest**. Then underline the **est** part of the word: **strongest**.
2. Ask the children to underline the **est** spelling pattern in all of the words in the Word Bank.

Pupil Book Activity 3: Circle the consonant letters

1. Ask the children to tell you what the consonant letters are (**b, c, d, f, g, h, j, k, l, m, n, p, q, r, s, t, v, w, x, y, z**). Remind the children of the spelling rule – that if the word ends in two consonant letters the **-est** ending is simply added on.
2. Ask the children to go back through the words in the Word Bank and this time use a coloured pen or pencil to circle the consonant letters that come before the **-est** pattern. Ask the children if all of the words have two consonant letters before the **-est** pattern. (No, they do not, for example, **weakest**)

Pupil Book Activity 4: Complete the Sentences

1. Read sentences **a – e** to the children, pausing as you reach each gap. Complete the first sentence with the children by re-reading to the first gap and then say: Look at the words in the Word Bank. Elicit children's ideas and establish that the word that fill the gap well is **neatest**.
2. Ask the children to fill in the gaps in the rest of the sentences independently or with a partner.

Answers: a) neatest; b) freshest; c) fastest; d) youngest; e) brightest

Pupil Book Activity 5: Challenge!

1. Set the children the challenge of writing their own short story using **–est** words. Explain to the children that using the words in this way will help them to remember the words more effectively. Encourage the children to include as many of the Word Bank words as possible.
2. Use the following text as a model to show the children how to write the short story or, alternatively, use the text as a passage dictation by reading each sentence slowly and clearly for the children to write down:

Dragon Class decided to see who the **greatest** student was. They held a race to see who would be the **fastest** student. They looked at each others' desks to see who was the **neatest** and **cleanest**. The teacher looked in the register to see who the **youngest** student was. Finally she looked at their smiles to see who the **brightest** student was.

Watch Out!

1. Draw the children's attention to the Watch Out! box at the bottom of the page.
2. Explain to the children that when we add **–est** to words ending in **e**, we drop the **e**.
3. Show the following examples on the board or point them out in the Pupil Book, **brave – bravest**, **wise – wisest**.

Assessment: -est, Tricky Words

Tell the children that you are going to read out ten words, one at a time. Each word will be one of the **-est** or tricky words that they have been learning. Tell the children that you will say the word, and then you will read out a sentence containing the word to help them know what it means. You will then repeat the word on its own before pausing so that the children can write the word down. For example: 1. **freshest**. The bread was at its **freshest** in the morning. **freshest**.

1. **freshest**. The bread was at its **freshest** in the morning. **freshest**
2. **was**. I **was** waiting all day. **was**
3. **fastest**. Tom was the **fastest** runner in the race. **fastest**
4. **today**. The weather was lovely **today**. **today**
5. **strongest**. Faye is the **strongest** person in our class. **strongest**
6. **weakest**. George is the **weakest** in the class. **weakest**
7. **you**. I would like to invite **you** over for tea. **you**
8. **grandest**. We went to the **grandest** museum of all. **grandest**
9. **said**. Mum **said** we could go to the toy shop. **said**
10. **are**. Rav and Deb **are** going to the match. **are**

For those students who need a bit more of a spelling challenge, read out the five further 'Quiet Zone' words to spell: **youngest**, **brightest**, **were**, **your**, **they**.

STATION - WEEK 9
Rainy Way

OBJECTIVES
PART 1 – ai
Spell and use words in writing containing **ai**

Review previous learning

Ask the children if they can recall the spelling rule or any example words from the previous spelling lesson. Elicit ideas and remind the children that: The ending **–est** always adds an extra syllable to the word. If the adjective ends in two consonant letters (the same or different), the ending is simply added on, for example, **quickest**, **smartest**.

Introducing the rule

Explain to the children that in today's lesson they will learn about words that are spelt with **ai**.

The digraph **ai** is virtually never used at the end of English words.

> **Optional: Review the Letterland character stories**
> Character-based stories can help children to remember spelling patterns (see page 121).

Pupil Book Activity 1: Picture Match

1. Draw children's attention to the Word Bank at the top of page 18. Explain that all of these words contain **ai**.
2. Ask the children to read through the words in the Word Bank and talk to a partner about what they mean. Then ask the children if there are any words they are unsure of and explain the meanings to them, looking in the dictionary for a definition if necessary.
3. Ask the children to find and copy words from the Word Bank to match the pictures.

Answers: a) snail; b) paint; c) chain; d) rain; e) aim; f) train

Pupil Book Activity 2: Underline ai

1. Model the activity by choosing a word from the Word Bank and writing it on the board, for example: **rain**. Then underline the **ai** part of the word: **r<u>ai</u>n**
2. Ask the children to underline the **ai** spelling pattern in all of the words in the Word Bank. Ask: Does the **ai** pattern always come in the middle of the words? (Yes, any examples where it does not are very rare, for example, **ch<u>ai</u>** and **samur<u>ai</u>** which are not rooted in English).

Pupil Book Activity 3: Complete the Sentences

1. Read sentences **a – e** to the children, pausing as you reach each gap. Complete the first sentence with the children by re-reading to the first gap and then say: Look at the Word Bank. Which word is something that might make you wet? Elicit children's ideas and establish that the word is **rain**.
2. Ask the children to fill in the gaps in the rest of the sentences independently or with a partner.

Answers: a) rain; b) tail; c) snail; d) paint; e) wait

Pupil Book Activity 4: Challenge!

1. Set the children the challenge of writing their own short story using **ai** words. Explain to the children that using the words in this way will help them to remember the words more effectively. Encourage the children to include as many of the Word Bank words as possible.

2. Use the following text as a model to show the children how to write the short story or, alternatively, use the text as a passage dictation by reading each sentence slowly and clearly for the children to write down:

Kelly stood in the **rain**. She had been told to **wait** for the **train**. She had **paid** for her ticket but was **afraid** the **train** was not coming. Her **aim** was to get to the next town. There she was going to **paint** a **chain** on the side of a boat.

> **OBJECTIVES**
> **PART 2 – ay**
> **Spell and use words in writing containing ay**

Review previous learning

Ask the children if they can recall the spelling rule or any example words from the previous spelling lesson. Elicit ideas and remind the children that: The digraph **ai** is virtually never used at the end of English words.

Introducing the rule

Explain to the children that in today's lesson they will learn about words that are spelt with **ay**.

The digraph **ay** is used at the end of words and at the end of syllables.

Optional: Review the Letterland character stories
Character-based stories can help children to remember spelling patterns (see page 121).

Pupil Book Activity 1: Picture Match

1. Draw the children's attention to the Word Bank at the top of page 19. Explain that all of these words contain **ay**.
2. Ask the children to read through the words in the Word Bank and talk to a partner about what they mean. Then ask the children if there are any words they are unsure of and explain the meanings to them, looking in the dictionary for a definition if necessary.
3. Ask the children to find and copy words from the Word Bank to match the pictures.

Answers: a) crayon; b) spray; c) holiday

Pupil Book Activity 2: Word Match

1. Draw the children's attention to the words written underneath the blank drawing boxes.
2. Ask the children to read each word and talk to a partner about what they mean.
3. Ask the children to draw a simple picture to match the words underneath each box, for example, to match the word 'play', children could draw themselves playing a favourite game.

Pupil Book Activity 3: Complete the Sentences

1. Read sentences **a – e** to the children, pausing as you reach each gap. Complete the first sentence with the children by re-reading to the first gap and then say: *Look at the Word Bank. Which word is something you might want to do at the library?* Elicit the children's ideas and establish that the word is **stay**.
2. Ask the children to fill in the gaps in the rest of the sentences independently or with a partner.

Answers: a) stay; b) clay; c) holiday; d) tray; e) crayon

Pupil Book Activity 4: Challenge!

1. Draw the children's attention to the Word Search at the bottom of page 19. Set children the challenge of finding ten **ai** and **ay** words in the Word Search. Eight of the words run horizontally from left to right and two words run vertically from top to bottom.
2. Tell the children to circle each word as they find it and then write the words in the correct column.

Answers:

h	o	l	i	d	a	y	e
r	a	i	n	c	h	n	p
b	g	s	n	a	i	l	l
a	t	r	a	i	n	s	a
t	r	a	y	m	j	p	y
a	f	r	a	i	d	r	f
p	a	i	n	t	k	a	l
c	r	a	y	o	n	y	d

ai	ay
rain	holiday
snail	play
train	spray
afraid	tray
paint	crayon

Assessment: ai, ay

Tell the children that you are going to read out ten words, one at a time. Each word will be one of the **ai** or **ay** words that they have been learning. Tell the children that you will say the word, and then you will read out a sentence containing the word to help them know what it means. You will then repeat the word on its own before pausing so that the children can write the word down. For example: 1. **rain**. I wear my coat in the **rain**. **rain**

1. **rain**. I wear my coat in the **rain**. **rain**
2. **wait**. I **wait** for the bus after school. **wait**
3. **away**. The dark clouds have blown **away**. **away**
4. **train**. I like to travel by **train**. **train**
5. **clay**. We have fun making things with **clay**. **clay**
6. **paid**. We **paid** at the till for our shopping. **paid**
7. **day**. My sister is starting school on this **day**. **day**
8. **aim**. I took **aim** with my bow and arrow set. **aim**
9. **play**. We went outside to **play**. **play**
10. **stay**. I asked my aunt if she could **stay** for longer. **stay**

For those students who need a bit more of a spelling challenge, read out the five further 'Quiet Zone' words to spell: **afraid, chain, crayon, holiday, spray**.

Full details of how to carry out assessment can be found on pages 6 and 108 of this guide.

STATION - WEEK 10

Lake Scene

OBJECTIVES
PART 1 – a_e
Spell and use words in writing containing a_e

Review previous learning

Ask the children if they can recall the spelling rule or any example words from the previous spelling lesson. Elicit ideas and remind the children that: The digraph **ay** is used for that sound at the end of words and at the end of syllables.

Introducing the rule

Explain to the children that in today's lesson they will learn about words that are spelt with **a_e**.

The long vowel sound /ay/ can be spelt in many different ways. For example, **ai** as in **rain**, **ay** as in **play** and **a_e** as in **cake**.

Optional: **Review the Letterland character stories**

Character-based stories can help children to remember spelling patterns (see page 122).

Pupil Book Activity 1: Picture Match

1. Draw children's attention to the Word Bank at the top of page 20. Explain that all of these words contain **a_e**.
2. Ask the children to read through the words in the Word Bank and talk to a partner about what they mean. Then ask the children if there are any words they are unsure of and explain the meanings to them, looking in the dictionary for a definition if necessary.
3. Highlight and discuss the different possible meanings of the word **safe** (to feel safe; to put valuables inside a safe).
4. Ask the children to find and copy words from the Word Bank to match the pictures.

Answers: a) spade; b) grape; c) plate; d) cake; e) cave; f) gate

Pupil Book Activity 2: Underline a_e

1. Model the activity by choosing a word from the Word Bank and writing it on the board, for example: **cake**. Then underline the **a_e** part of the word: **cake**
2. Ask the children to underline the **a_e** spelling pattern in all of the words in the Word Bank.

Pupil Book Activity 3: Complete the Sentences

1. Read sentences **a – e** to the children, pausing as you reach each gap. Complete the first sentence with the children by re-reading to the first gap and then say: Look at the Word Bank. Which word is somewhere a banker might put money? Elicit children's ideas and establish that the word is **safe**.
2. Ask the children to fill in the gaps in the rest of the sentences independently or with a partner.

Answers: a) safe; b) case; c) gate; d) stale; e) rake

Pupil Book Activity 4: Challenge!

1. Set the children the challenge of writing their own short story using **a_e** words. Explain to the children that using the words in this way will help them to remember the words more effectively.

Encourage the children to include as many of the Word Bank words as possible.

2. Use the following text as a model to show the children how to write the short story or, alternatively, use the text as a passage dictation by reading each sentence slowly and clearly for the children to write down:

Mrs Smith put the **cake** inside her **case**. She tidied the **rake** and **spade** in to the garden shed. Then she left through the open **gate**. When she got to the **cave** she took out a **plate** and some **grapes**. She ate some **cake** but it was a bit **stale**.

Review previous learning

Ask the children if they can recall the spelling rule or any example words from the previous spelling lesson. Elicit ideas and remind the children that: The long vowel sound /ay/ can be spelt in many different ways. For example, **ai** as in **rain**, **ay** as in **play** and **a_e** as in **cake**.

> **OBJECTIVES**
> **PART 2 – e_e**
> Spell and use words in writing containing e_e

Introducing the rule

Explain to the children that in today's lesson they will learn about words that are spelt with **e_e**.

The long vowel sound /ee/ can be spelt in many different ways. For example, **ee** as in **feet**, **ea** as in **seat** and **e_e** as in **athlete**.

> **Optional: Review the Letterland character stories**
> Character-based stories can help children to remember spelling patterns (see page 122).

Pupil Book Activity 1: Picture Match

1. Draw the children's attention to the Word Bank at the top of page 21. Explain that all of these words contain **e_e**.
2. Ask the children to read through the words in the Word Bank and talk to a partner about what they mean. Then ask the children if there are any words they are unsure of and explain the meanings to them, looking in the dictionary for a definition if necessary. The Word Bank for the **e_e** spellings is an ambitious one and you may need to spend a little more time ensuring that you teach and discuss the meanings of the words.
3. Ask the children to find and copy words from the Word Bank to match the pictures.

Answers: a) delete; b) trapeze; c) compete

Pupil Book Activity 2: Word Match

1. Draw the children's attention to the words written underneath the blank drawing boxes.
2. Ask the children to read each word and talk to a partner about what they mean.
3. Ask the children to draw a simple picture to match the words underneath each box, for example, to match the word 'complete', children could draw themselves with a medal.

Pupil Book Activity 3: Complete the Sentences

1. Read sentences **a – e** to the children, pausing as you reach each gap. Complete the first sentence with the children by re-reading to the first gap and then say: *Look at the Word Bank. Which word is something a path might be made from?* Elicit ideas and establish that the word is **concrete**.
2. Ask the children to fill in the gaps in the rest of the sentences independently or with a partner.

Answers: a) concrete; b) trapeze; c) theme; d) extreme; e) scene

Pupil Book Activity 4: Challenge!

1. Draw the children's attention to the Word Search at the bottom of page 21. Set children the challenge of finding ten **a_e** and **e_e** words in the Word Search. Eight of the words run horizontally from left to right and two words run vertically from top to bottom.
2. Tell the children to circle each word as they find it and then write the words in two columns. *Answers:*

c	o	m	p	e	t	e	t
r	a	k	e	d	i	c	h
j	d	e	l	e	t	e	e
c	k	o	g	a	t	e	m
a	p	l	a	t	e	h	e
k	n	s	t	a	l	e	g
e	b	m	t	h	e	s	e
a	s	c	e	n	e	f	l

a_e	e_e
rake	compete
gate	delete
cake	theme
plate	these
stale	scene

Assessment: a_e, e_e

Tell the children that you are going to read out ten words, one at a time. Each word will be one of the **a_e** or **e_e** words that they have been learning. Tell the children that you will say the word, and then you will read out a sentence containing the word to help them know what it means. You will then repeat the word on its own before pausing so that the children can write the word down. For example:
1. **cake**. I love chocolate **cake**. **cake**

1. **cake**. I love chocolate **cake**. **cake**
2. **compete**. Our class is going to **compete** in the competition. **compete**
3. **delete**. I accidentally pressed **delete**. **delete**
4. **case**. I have a new **case** for my trip. **case**
5. **rake**. We will **rake** up the fallen leaves. **rake**
6. **theme**. The festival **theme** is happiness. **theme**
7. **athlete**. We met a famous **athlete**. **athlete**
8. **gate**. My cat likes to sit on the **gate**. **gate**
9. **cave**. We explored the **cave**. **cave**
10. **these**. My mum gave us **these** sweets. **these**

For those students who need a bit more of a spelling challenge, read out the five further 'Quiet Zone' words to spell: **stale, grape, spade, trapeze, concrete**.

Full details of how to carry out assessment can be found on pages 6 and 108 of this guide.

STATION - WEEK 11

Bike Zone

OBJECTIVES
PART 1 – i_e
Spell and use words in writing containing i_e

Review previous learning

Ask the children if they can recall the spelling rule or any example words from the previous spelling lesson. Elicit ideas and remind the children that: The long vowel sound /ee/ can be spelt in many different ways. For example, **ee** as in **feet**, **ea** as in **seat** and **e_e** as in **athlete**.

Introducing the rule

Explain to the children that in today's lesson they will learn about words that are spelt with **i_e**.

The long vowel sound /igh/ can be spelt in many different ways. For example, **ie** as in **tie**, **igh** as in **night**, **i_e** as in **bike** and **y** as in **cry**.

> **Optional: Review the Letterland character stories**
> Character-based stories can help children to remember spelling patterns (see page 122).

Pupil Book Activity 1: Picture Match

1. Draw children's attention to the Word Bank at the top of page 22. Explain that all of these words contain **i_e**.
2. Ask the children to read through the words in the Word Bank and talk to a partner about what they mean. Then ask the children if there are any words they are unsure of and explain the meanings to them, looking in the dictionary for a definition if necessary.
3. Ask the children to find and copy words from the Word Bank to match the pictures.

Answers: a) kite; b) slide; c) bike; d) fire; e) knife; f) five

Pupil Book Activity 2: Underline i_e

1. Model the activity by choosing a word from the Word Bank and writing it on the board, for example: **bike**. Then underline the **i_e** part of the word: **bike**
2. Ask the children to underline the **i_e** spelling pattern in all of the words in the Word Bank.

Pupil Book Activity 3: Complete the Sentences

1. Read sentences **a** – **e** to the children, pausing as you reach each gap. Complete the first sentence with the children by re-reading to the first gap and then say: Look at the Word Bank. Which word is something you might get if you come first in a competition? Elicit children's ideas and establish that the word is **prize**.
2. Ask the children to fill in the gaps in the rest of the sentences independently or with a partner.

Answers: a) prize; b) bike; c) time; d) slide; e) kite

Pupil Book Activity 4: Challenge!

1. Set the children the challenge of writing their own short story using **i_e** words. Explain to the children that using the words in this way will help them to remember the words more effectively. Encourage the children to include as many of the Word Bank words as possible.

2. Use the following text as a model to show the children how to write the short story or, alternatively, use the text as a passage dictation by reading each sentence slowly and clearly for the children to write down:

Hassan rode his **bike** to the park. Kate took her **kite**. Altogether there were **nine** friends at the park so they had a big game of **hide** and seek. At **five** o'clock it was **time** to go home. They both had a quick turn down the **slide** before they left.

Review previous learning

Ask the children if they can recall the spelling rule or any example words from the previous spelling lesson. Elicit ideas and remind the children that: The long vowel sound /igh/ can be spelt in many different ways. For example, **ie** as in **tie**, **igh** as in **night**, **i_e** as in **bike** and **y** as in **cry**.

> **OBJECTIVES**
> **PART 2 – o_e**
> Spell and use words in writing containing o_e

Introducing the rule

Explain to the children that in today's lesson they will learn about words that are spelt with **o_e**.

The long vowel sound /oa/ can be spelt in many different ways. For example, **oa** as in **coat**, **o_e** as in **rose** and **ow** as in **snow**.

Optional: Review the Letterland character stories

Character-based stories can help children to remember spelling patterns (see page 122).

Pupil Book Activity 1: Picture Match

1. Draw the children's attention to the Word Bank at the top of page 23. Explain that all of these words contain **o_e**.
2. Ask the children to read through the words in the Word Bank and talk to a partner about what they mean. Then ask the children if there are any words they are unsure of and explain the meanings to them, looking in the dictionary for a definition if necessary.
3. Ask the children to find and copy words from the Word Bank to match the pictures.

Answers: a) cone; b) rose; c) globe

Pupil Book Activity 2: Word Match

1. Draw the children's attention to the words written underneath the blank drawing boxes.
2. Ask the children to read each word and talk to a partner about what they mean.
3. Ask the children to draw a simple picture to match the words underneath each box, for example, to match the word 'home', children could draw a picture of their own home.

Pupil Book Activity 3: Complete the Sentences

1. Read sentences **a – e** to the children, pausing as you reach each gap. Complete the first sentence with the children by re-reading to the first gap and then say: Look at the Word Bank. Which word is something you can talk to someone with? Elicit the children's ideas and establish that the word is **phone**.
2. Ask the children to fill in the gaps in the rest of the sentences independently or with a partner.

Answers: a) phone; b) globe; c) note; d) poke; e) hope

Pupil Book Activity 4: Challenge!

1. Draw the children's attention to the Word Search at the bottom of page 23. Set children the challenge of finding ten **i_e** and **o_e** words in the Word Search. Eight of the words run horizontally from left to right and two words run vertically from top to bottom.
2. Tell the children to circle each word as they find it and then write the words in two columns.

Answers:

b	i	k	e	q	t	k	e
i	p	c	o	n	e	r	s
p	t	i	m	e	j	a	m
o	b	h	f	h	o	p	e
k	g	l	o	b	e	d	f
e	n	o	k	i	t	e	i
u	s	l	i	d	e	l	v
p	h	o	n	e	c	g	e

i_e	o_e
bike	cone
time	poke
five	hope
slide	globe
kite	phone

Assessment: i_e, o_e

Tell the children that you are going to read out ten words, one at a time. Each word will be one of the **i_e** or **o_e** words that they have been learning. Tell the children that you will say the word, and then you will read out a sentence containing the word to help them know what it means. You will then repeat the word on its own before pausing so that the children can write the word down. For example: 1. **five**. I eat my dinner at **five** o'clock. **five**

1. **five**. I eat my dinner at **five** o'clock. **five**
2. **cone**. Dan ate an ice cream in a **cone**. **cone**
3. **bike**. My **bike** is red and blue. **bike**
4. **rose**. Dad planted a **rose** bush. **rose**
5. **kite**. We flew our **kite** last weekend. **kite**
6. **home**. We welcome friends to our **home**. **home**
7. **nine**. My brother is **nine** years old. **nine**
8. **globe**. I found our country on the **globe**. **globe**
9. **hide**. My cat likes to **hide** in boxes. **hide**
10. **bone**. My mum gave the dog a **bone**. **bone**

For those students who need a bit more of a spelling challenge, read out the five further 'Quiet Zone' words to spell: **prize**, **knife**, **slide**, **phone**, **broke**.

Full details of how to carry out assessment can be found on pages 6 and 108 of this guide.

STATION - WEEK 12

Huge Sheep

OBJECTIVES

PART 1 – u_e

Spell and use words in writing containing u_e

Review previous learning

Ask the children if they can recall the spelling rule or any example words from the previous spelling lesson. Elicit ideas and remind the children that: The long vowel sound /oa/ can be spelt in many different ways. For example, **oa** as in **coat**, **o_e** as in **rose** and **ow** as in **snow**.

Introducing the rule

Explain to the children that in today's lesson they will learn about words that are spelt with **u_e**.

Both the /oo/ and the /y+oo/ sounds can be spelt as **u_e**.

Optional: **Review the Letterland character stories**

Character-based stories can help children to remember spelling patterns (see page 122).

Pupil Book Activity 1: Picture Match

1. Draw children's attention to the Word Bank at the top of page 24. Explain that all of these words contain **u_e**.
2. Ask the children to read through the words in the Word Bank and talk to a partner about what they mean. Then ask the children if there are any words they are unsure of and explain the meanings to them, looking in the dictionary for a definition if necessary.
3. Ask the children to find and copy words from the Word Bank to match the pictures.

Answers: a) tube; b) flute; c) huge; d) tune; e) June; f) cube

Pupil Book Activity 2: Underline u_e

1. Model the activity by choosing a word from the Word Bank and writing it on the board, for example: tune. Then underline the **u_e** part of the word: **tune**
2. Ask the children to underline the **u_e** spelling pattern in all of the words in the Word Bank.

Pupil Book Activity 3: Check the sounds

1. Ask the children to re-read the words in the Word Bank either by themselves or with you. Discuss which words contain the /oo/sound and which words contain the /y+oo/ sound.
2. Ask the children to circle the words in the Word Bank that have the /oo/ sound and tick the words in the Word Bank that have the /y+oo/ sound.

Pupil Book Activity 4: Complete the Sentences

1. Read sentences **a – e** to the children, pausing as you reach each gap. Complete the first sentence with the children by re-reading to the first gap and then say: Look at the Word Bank. Which word is a time that somebody could have their birthday? Elicit children's ideas and establish that the word is **June**.
2. Ask the children to fill in the gaps in the rest of the sentences independently or with a partner.

Answers: a) June; b) flute; c) cute; d) rude; e) tune

Pupil Book Activity 4: Challenge!

1. Set the children the challenge of writing their own short story using **u_e** words. Explain to the children that using the words in this way will help them to remember the words more effectively. Encourage the children to include as many of the Word Bank words as possible.

2. Use the following text as a model to show the children how to write the short story or, alternatively, use the text as a passage dictation by reading each sentence slowly and clearly for the children to write down:

Mary started to play the **flute** in **June**. By July she could play three **tunes**. Her **cute** baby brother **used** a **tube** to pretend to play the **flute** too.

Review previous learning

Ask the children if they can recall the spelling rule or any example words from the previous spelling lesson. Elicit ideas and remind the children that: Both the /oo/ and the /y+oo/ sounds can be spelt as **u_e**.

> **OBJECTIVES**
> **PART 2 - ee**
> Spell and use words containing **ee** in their own writing

Introducing the rule

Explain to the children that in today's lesson they will learn about words that are spelt with **ee**.

The long vowel sound /ee/ can be spelt in many different ways. For example, **ea** as in **seat**, **y** as in **baby**, **ie** as in **field** and **ee** as in **feet**.

> **Optional: Review the Letterland character stories**
> Character-based stories can help children to remember spelling patterns (see page 122).

Pupil Book Activity 1: Picture Match

1. Draw the children's attention to the Word Bank at the top of page 25. Explain that all of these words contain **ee**.
2. Ask the children to read through the words in the Word Bank and talk to a partner about what they mean. Then ask the children if there are any words they are unsure of and explain the meanings to them, looking in the dictionary for a definition if necessary.
3. Ask the children to find and copy words from the Word Bank to match the pictures.

Answers: a) bee; b) knee; c) sleep

Pupil Book Activity 2: Word Match

1. Draw the children's attention to the words written underneath the blank drawing boxes.
2. Ask the children to read each word and talk to a partner about what they mean.
3. Ask the children to draw a simple picture to match the words underneath each box, for example, to match the word 'three', children could draw three flowers or three smiley faces.

Pupil Book Activity 3: Complete the Sentences

1. Read sentences **a – e** to the children, pausing as you reach each gap. Complete the first sentence with the children by re-reading to the first gap and then say: Look at the Word Bank. Which word describes how grass looks? Elicit the children's ideas and establish that the word is **green**.
2. Ask the children to fill in the gaps in the rest of the sentences independently or with a partner.

Answers: a) green; b) teeth; c) sheep; d) sleep; e) knee

Pupil Book Activity 4: Challenge!

1. Draw the children's attention to the Word Search at the bottom of page 25. Set children the challenge of finding ten **u_e** and **ee** words in the Word Search. Eight of the words run horizontally from left to right and two words run vertically from top to bottom.
2. Tell the children to circle each word as they find it and then write the words in two columns.

Answers:

f	l	u	t	e	f	p	k
a	q	g	l	c	u	b	e
t	s	h	e	e	p	s	v
u	m	r	k	n	e	e	b
b	o	h	u	g	e	t	r
e	t	h	r	e	e	j	u
n	u	g	r	e	e	n	l
h	b	e	e	c	d	i	e

u_e	ee
flute	sheep
cube	knee
rule	three
tube	green
huge	bee

Assessment: u_e, ee

Tell the children that you are going to read out ten words, one at a time. Each word will be one of the **u_e** or **ee** words that they have been learning. Tell the children that you will say the word, and then you will read out a sentence containing the word to help them know what it means. You will then repeat the word on its own before pausing so that the children can write the word down. For example:
1. **rude**. Poking your tongue out is **rude**. **rude**

1. **rude**. Poking your tongue out is **rude**. **rude**
2. **sheep**. We saw some **sheep** in the field. **sheep**
3. **tune**. I can play a **tune**. **tune**
4. **flute**. I am learning to play the **flute**. **flute**
5. **green**. The grass is the colour **green**. **green**
6. **cube**. A **cube** is a 3D shape. **cube**
7. **three**. I have **three** new books. **three**
8. **sleep**. My cat likes to **sleep** by the fire. **sleep**
9. **June**. We are going on holiday in **June**. **June**
10. **bee**. The **bee** was sitting on the flower. **bee**

For those students who need a bit more of a spelling challenge, read out the five further 'Quiet Zone' words to spell: **brute**, **plume**, **agree**, **knee**, **teeth**.

Full details of how to carry out assessment can be found on pages 6 and 108 of this guide.

STATION - WEEK 13

Beach Head

OBJECTIVES

PART 1 - ea

Spell and use words containing **ea** in writing

Review previous learning

Ask the children if they can recall the spelling rule or any example words from the previous spelling lesson. Elicit ideas and remind the children that: The long vowel sound /ee/ can be spelt in many different ways. For example, **ea** as in **seat**, **ie** as in **field**, **y** as in **baby** and **ee** as in **feet**.

Introducing the rule

Explain to the children that in today's lesson they will learn about words that are spelt with **ea**.

The long vowel sound /ee/ can be spelt in many different ways. For example, **ea** as in **seat**, **ie** as in **field**, **y** as in **baby** and **ee** as in **feet**.

> **Optional: Review the Letterland character stories**
>
> Character-based stories can help children to remember spelling patterns (see page 122).

Pupil Book Activity 1: Picture Match

1. Draw children's attention to the Word Bank at the top of page 26. Explain that all of these words contain **ea**.
2. Ask the children to read through the words in the Word Bank and talk to a partner about what they mean. Then ask the children if there are any words they are unsure of and explain the meanings to them, looking in the dictionary for a definition if necessary.
3. Highlight and discuss the meaning of the word 'sea' compared to the meaning and spelling of 'see'. Highlight and discuss the different meanings of the word 'seal' (the animal and 'to seal' a box shut).
4. Ask the children to find and copy words from the Word Bank to match the pictures.

Answers: a) leaf; b) peach; c) bean; d) seal; e) dream; f) sea

Pupil Book Activity 2: Underline ea

1. Model the activity by choosing a word from the Word Bank and writing it on the board, for example: **leaf**. Then underline the **ea** part of the word: l**ea**f.
2. Ask the children to underline the **ea** spelling pattern in all of the words in the Word Bank.

Pupil Book Activity 3: Complete the Sentences

1. Read sentences **a – e** to the children, pausing as you reach each gap. Complete the first sentence with the children by re-reading to the first gap and then say: *Look at the Word Bank. Which word is something green on which you might see a bug?* Elicit children's ideas and establish that the word is **leaf**.
2. Ask the children to fill in the gaps in the rest of the sentences independently or with a partner.

Answers: a) leaf; b) peach; c) dream; d) seal; e) reach

Pupil Book Activity 4: Challenge!

1. Set the children the challenge of writing their own short story using **ea** words. Explain to the children that using the words in this way will help them to remember the words more effectively. Encourage the children to include as many of the Word Bank words as possible.

2. Use the following text as a model to show the children how to write the short story or, alternatively, use the text as a passage dictation by reading each sentence slowly and clearly for the children to write down:

Liam had a **dream** that he was at the **beach** on holiday. He paddled in the **sea** and saw a **seal**. He asked his Mum for a **peach** and remembered to say **please**.

Review previous learning

Ask the children if they can recall the spelling rule or any example words from the previous spelling lesson. Elicit ideas and remind the children that: The long vowel sound /ee/ can be spelt in many different ways. For example, **ea** as in **seat**, **ie** as in **field**, **y** as in **baby** and **ee** as in **feet**.

> **OBJECTIVES**
> **PART 2 – ea**
> Spell and use words in writing containing **ea**

Introducing the rule

Explain to the children that in today's lesson they will learn about more words that are spelt with **ea**.

The letters **ea** can represent the sound /ee/ but they can also represent the sound /e/. For example, **head**, **bread**.

Optional: Review the Letterland character stories

Character-based stories can help children to remember spelling patterns (see page 122).

Pupil Book Activity 1: Picture Match

1. Draw the children's attention to the Word Bank at the top of page 27. Explain that all of these words contain **ea**.
2. Ask the children to read through the words in the Word Bank and talk to a partner about what they mean. Then ask the children if there are any words they are unsure of and explain the meanings to them, looking in the dictionary for a definition if necessary.
3. Ask the children to find and copy words from the Word Bank to match the pictures.

Answers: a) thread; b) ahead; c) tread

Pupil Book Activity 2: Word Match

1. Draw the children's attention to the words written underneath the blank drawing boxes.
2. Ask the children to read each word and talk to a partner about what they mean.
3. Ask the children to draw a simple picture to match the words underneath each box, for example, to match the word 'bread', children could draw a loaf of bread or a favourite sandwich.

Pupil Book Activity 3: Complete the Sentences

1. Read sentences **a – e** to the children, pausing as you reach each gap. Complete the first sentence with the children by re-reading to the first gap and then say: Look at the Word Bank. Which word is somewhere that you wear a hat? Elicit the children's ideas and establish that the word is **head**.

2. Ask the children to fill in the gaps in the rest of the sentences independently or with a partner.
Answers: a) head; b) read; c) thread; d) bread; e) instead

Pupil Book Activity 4: Challenge!

1. Draw the children's attention to the Word Search at the bottom of page 27. Set children the challenge of finding ten **ea** /ee/ and **ea** /e/ words in the Word Search. Eight of the words run horizontally from left to right and two words run vertically from top to bottom.
2. Tell the children to circle each word as they find it and then write the words in two columns.

Answers:

r	c	b	e	a	c	h	f
h	b	e	a	n	m	a	p
e	g	d	r	e	a	d	k
a	l	q	l	e	a	f	b
d	i	d	e	a	f	e	r
h	s	e	a	l	o	n	e
p	e	a	c	h	j	r	a
m	e	a	n	t	b	s	d

ea /ee/	ea /e/
beach	bread
leaf	meant
seal	head
peach	dread
bean	deaf

Assessment: ea /ee/, ea /e/

Tell the children that you are going to read out ten words, one at a time. Each word will be one of the **ea** /ee/ or **ea** /e/ words that they have been learning. Tell the children that you will say the word, and then you will read out a sentence containing the word to help them know what it means. You will then repeat the word on its own before pausing so that the children can write the word down. For example:
1. **sea**. I like to watch the boats at **sea**. **sea**

1. **sea**. I like to watch the boats at **sea**. **sea**
2. **bread**. I bake **bread** with Grandpa. **bread**
3. **leaf**. I saw a **leaf** in a lovely shape. **leaf**
4. **read**. I have already **read** that book. **read**
5. **peach**. The muffins have a **peach** flavor. **peach**
6. **head**. The butterfly landed on my **head**. **head**
7. **seal**. I saw a **seal** on the rocks. **seal**
8. **thread**. I am sewing with yellow **thread**. **thread**
9. **bean**. I shall plant this little **bean**. **bean**
10. **instead**. My mum gave us pasta **instead** of pizza. **instead**

For those students who need a bit more of a spelling challenge, read out the five further 'Quiet Zone' words to spell: **please, season, reach, ahead, dread**.

Full details of how to carry out assessment can be found on pages 6 and 108 of this guide.

STATION - WEEK 14
Field Farm

OBJECTIVES
PART 1 – ie

Spell and use words in writing containing **ie**

Review previous learning

Ask the children if they can recall the spelling rule or any example words from the previous spelling lesson. Elicit ideas and remind the children that: The letters **ea** can represent the sound /ee/ but they can also represent the sound /e/. For example, **head**, **bread**.

Introducing the rule

Explain to the children that in today's lesson they will learn about words that are spelt with **ie**.

The long vowel sound /ee/ can be spelt in many different ways. For example, **ea** as in **seat**, **ie** as in **field**, **y** as in **baby** and **ee** as in **feet**.

> **Optional: Review the Letterland character stories**
>
> Character-based stories can help children to remember spelling patterns (see page 122).

Pupil Book Activity 1: Picture Match

1. Draw children's attention to the Word Bank at the top of page 28. Explain that all of these words contain **ie**.
2. Ask the children to read through the words in the Word Bank and talk to a partner about what they mean. Then ask the children if there are any words they are unsure of and explain the meanings to them, looking in the dictionary for a definition if necessary.
3. Ask the children to find and copy words from the Word Bank to match the pictures.

Answers: a) movie; b) grief; c) field; d) piece; e) shield; f) chief

Pupil Book Activity 2: Underline ie

1. Model the activity by choosing a word from the Word Bank and writing it on the board, for example: **chief**. Then underline the **ie** part of the word: ch<u>ie</u>f.
2. Ask the children to underline the **ie** spelling pattern in all of the words in the Word Bank.

Pupil Book Activity 3: Complete the Sentences

1. Read sentences **a** – **e** to the children, pausing as you reach each gap. Complete the first sentence with the children by re-reading to the first gap and then say: Look at the Word Bank. Which word is another word meaning boss or leader? Elicit children's ideas and establish that the word is **chief**.
2. Ask the children to fill in the gaps in the rest of the sentences independently or with a partner.

Answers: a) chief; b) field; c) piece; d) movie; e) shield

Pupil Book Activity 4: Challenge!

1. Set the children the challenge of writing their own short story using **ie** words. Explain to the children that using the words in this way will help them to remember the words more effectively. Encourage the children to include as many of the Word Bank words as possible.

2. Use the following text as a model to show the children how to write the short story or, alternatively, use the text as a passage dictation by reading each sentence slowly and clearly for the children to write down:

Yanos played the part of a **chief** in a Roman tribe. He stood at the top of his **field** and held up his new **shield**. For a **brief** moment he felt like a **movie** star. He watched the other actors getting up to **mischief**.

Review previous learning

Ask the children if they can recall the spelling rule or any example words from the previous spelling lesson. Elicit ideas and remind the children that: The long vowel sound /ee/ can be spelt in many different ways. For example, **ea** as in **seat**, **ie** as in **field**, **y** as in **baby** and **ee** as in **feet**.

Introducing the rule

Explain to the children that in today's lesson they will learn about words that are spelt with **ar**.

The /ar/ sound can be spelt in different ways. For example, **al** as in **calm**, **a** as in **father** and **ar** as in **car**.

> **OBJECTIVES**
> **PART 2 – ar**
> Spell and use words in writing containing **ar**

Optional: Review the Letterland character stories

Character-based stories can help children to remember spelling patterns (see page 122).

Pupil Book Activity 1: Picture Match

1. Draw the children's attention to the Word Bank at the top of page 29. Explain that all of these words contain **ar**.
2. Ask the children to read through the words in the Word Bank and talk to a partner about what they mean. Then ask the children if there are any words they are unsure of and explain the meanings to them, looking in the dictionary for a definition if necessary.
3. Ask the children to find and copy words from the Word Bank to match the pictures.

Answers: a) market; b) jar; c) garden

Pupil Book Activity 2: Word Match

1. Draw the children's attention to the words written underneath the blank drawing boxes.
2. Ask the children to read each word and talk to a partner about what they mean.
3. Ask the children to draw a simple picture to match the words underneath each box, for example, to match the word 'car', children could draw their family car or their dream car.

Pupil Book Activity 3: Complete the Sentences

1. Read sentences **a – e** to the children, pausing as you reach each gap. Complete the first sentence with the children by re-reading to the first gap and then say: Look at the Word Bank. Which word is something that a family could have that has 7 seats? Elicit the children's ideas and establish that the word is **car**.
2. Ask the children to fill in the gaps in the rest of the sentences independently or with a partner.

Answers: a) car; b) March; c) bark; d) market; e) dark

Pupil Book Activity 4: Challenge!

1. Draw the children's attention to the Word Search at the bottom of page 29. Set children the challenge of finding ten **ie** and **ar** words in the Word Search. Eight of the words run horizontally from left to right and two words run vertically from top to bottom.
2. Tell the children to circle each word as they find it and then write the words in two columns.

Answers:

d	a	r	k	h	i	c	g
m	d	p	a	r	k	j	a
a	b	g	p	j	a	r	r
r	c	h	i	e	f	k	d
k	e	f	i	e	l	d	e
e	m	o	v	i	e	l	n
t	s	h	i	e	l	d	m
d	f	p	i	e	c	e	o

ie	ar
chief	dark
field	park
movie	garden
shield	market
piece	jar

Assessment: ie, ar

Tell the children that you are going to read out ten words, one at a time. Each word will be one of the **ie** or **ar** words that they have been learning. Tell the children that you will say the word, and then you will read out a sentence containing the word to help them know what it means. You will then repeat the word on its own before pausing so that the children can write the word down. For example:
1. **field**. The rice is growing in the **field**. **field**.

1. **field**. The rice is growing in the **field**. **field**
2. **thief**. The police caught the **thief**. **thief**
3. **star**. I saw a bright **star** in the night sky. **star**
4. **car**. Our family is getting a new **car**. **car**
5. **chief**. The town needed a new **chief**. **chief**
6. **piece**. I found the lost **piece** of my puzzle. **piece**
7. **shark**. I watched a show about a **shark**. **shark**
8. **March**. My favourite month is **March**. **March**
9. **movie**. We watched the new **movie**. **movie**
10. **park**. My mum took us to the **park**. **park**

For those students who need a bit more of a spelling challenge, read out the five further 'Quiet Zone' words to spell: **shield, mischief, garden, market, harvest**.

Full details of how to carry out assessment can be found on pages 6 and 108 of this guide.

STATION - WEEK 15

Herb Dinner

OBJECTIVES
PART 1 – er (stressed)
Spell and use words in writing containing **er**

Review previous learning

Ask the children if they can recall the spelling rule or any example words from the previous spelling lesson. Elicit ideas and remind the children that: The /ar/ sound can be spelt in different ways. For example, **al** as in **calm**, **a** as in **father** and **ar** as in **car**

Introducing the rule

Explain to the children that in today's lesson they will learn about words that are spelt with **er**.

In some words the spelling pattern **er** sounds like /er/. For example, **herb**. This is a stressed syllable. In other words the **er** spelling pattern is unstressed. It sounds like /u/. For example, **sister**.

Optional: Review the Letterland character stories

Character-based stories can help children to remember spelling patterns (see page 122).

Pupil Book Activity 1: Picture Match

1. Draw children's attention to the Word Bank at the top of page 30. Explain that all of these words contain **er**.
2. Ask the children to read through the words in the Word Bank and talk to a partner about what they mean. Then ask the children if there are any words they are unsure of and explain the meanings to them, looking in the dictionary for a definition if necessary.
3. Ask the children to find and copy words from the Word Bank to match the pictures.

Answers: a) emergency; b) herb; c) mermaid; d) person; e) perfume; f) her

Pupil Book Activity 2: Underline er

1. Model the activity by choosing a word from the Word Bank and writing it on the board, for example: **emergency**. Then underline the **er** part of the word: **em<u>er</u>gency**
2. Ask the children to underline the **er** spelling pattern in all of the words in the Word Bank.

Pupil Book Activity 3: Complete the Sentences

1. Read sentences **a – e** to the children, pausing as you reach each gap. Complete the first sentence with the children by re-reading to the first gap and then say: *Look at the Word Bank. Which word is an underwater creature from stories?* Elicit children's ideas and establish that the word is **mermaid**.
2. Ask the children to fill in the gaps in the rest of the sentences independently or with a partner.

Answers: a) mermaid; b) perfume; c) emergency; d) herb; e) verb

Pupil Book Activity 4: Challenge!

1. Set the children the challenge of writing their own short story using **er** words. Explain to the children that using the words in this way will help them to remember the words more effectively. Encourage the children to include as many of the Word Bank words as possible.

2. Use the following text as a model to show the children how to write the short story or, alternatively, use the text as a passage dictation by reading each sentence slowly and clearly for the children to write down:

Something was making **her** sneeze. It was either the **perfume** or the **herbs** in the curry. It felt like an **emergency**. To calm her **nerves** she read a story about a **mermaid** who wanted to become a human **person.**

Watch Out!

Draw children's attention to the Watch Out! box at the bottom of page 30. Explain to the children that the sound /er/ can be spelt in many different ways. For example, **er** as in **herb**, **ir** as in **bird**, **ur** as in **curl** and **or** as in **world**.

Review previous learning

Ask the children if they can recall the spelling rule or any example words from the previous spelling lesson. Elicit ideas and remind the children that: In some words the spelling pattern **er** sounds like /er/. For example, **herb**. This is a stressed syllable.

OBJECTIVES
PART 2 – er (unstressed)
Spell and use words in writing containing er

Introducing the rule

Explain to the children that in today's lesson they will learn about words that are spelt with **er**.

In some words the **er** spelling pattern is unstressed. Sometimes we call it a 'schwa'. It sounds like /u/. For example, **sister**.

Pupil Book Activity 1: Picture Match

1. Draw the children's attention to the Word Bank at the top of page 31. Explain that all of these words contain **er**.
2. Ask the children to read through the words in the Word Bank and talk to a partner about what they mean. Then ask the children if there are any words they are unsure of and explain the meanings to them, looking in the dictionary for a definition if necessary.
3. Ask the children to find and copy words from the Word Bank to match the pictures.

Answers: a) flower; b) under; c) winter

Pupil Book Activity 2: Word Match

1. Draw the children's attention to the words written underneath the blank drawing boxes.
2. Ask the children to read each word and talk to a partner about what they mean.
3. Ask the children to draw a simple picture to match the words underneath each box, for example, to match the word 'mother', children could draw their own mother.

Pupil Book Activity 3: Complete the Sentences

1. Read sentences **a – e** to the children, pausing as you reach each gap. Complete the first sentence with the children by re-reading to the first gap and then say: Look at the Word Bank. If a cat wanted to hide in a room with one chair, would it sit *on* the chair or sit somewhere else? Elicit the children's ideas and establish that the word is **under**.
2. Ask the children to fill in the gaps in the rest of the sentences independently or with a partner.

Answers: a) under; b) flower; c) hotter; d) sister; e) faster

Pupil Book Activity 4: Challenge!

1. Draw the children's attention to the Word Search at the bottom of page 31. Set children the challenge of finding ten **er** (stressed) and **er** (unstressed) words in the Word Search. Eight of the words run horizontally from left to right and two words run vertically from top to bottom.
2. Tell the children to circle each word as they find it and then write the words in two columns.

Answers:

f	a	s	t	e	r	i	h
f	e	u	n	d	e	r	o
l	n	e	r	v	e	f	t
o	p	e	r	s	o	n	t
w	h	e	r	b	h	g	e
e	a	l	e	r	t	j	r
r	d	t	e	r	m	c	k
a	s	i	s	t	e	r	b

er (stressed)	er (unstressed)
nerve	faster
person	flower
alert	hotter
term	under
herb	sister

Assessment: er, er

Tell the children that you are going to read out ten words, one at a time. Each word will be one of the **er** (stressed) or **er** (unstressed) words that they have been learning. Tell the children that you will say the word, and then you will read out a sentence containing the word to help them know what it means. You will then repeat the word on its own before pausing so that the children can write the word down. For example: 1. **herb**. I grew a new **herb** in the garden. **herb**

1. **herb**. I grew a new **herb** in the garden. **herb**
2. **teacher**. Our **teacher** helps us learn. **teacher**
3. **person**. I met a new **person**. **person**
4. **winter**. I wrap up warm in **winter**. **winter**
5. **mermaid**. I wrote a story about a **mermaid**. **mermaid**
6. **summer**. The **summer** is hot here. **summer**
7. **term**. The school **term** has almost ended. **term**
8. **her**. I am going to **her** house after school. **her**
9. **under**. I snuggled **under** the blanket. **under**
10. **sister**. I have an older **sister**. **sister**

For those students who need a bit more of a spelling challenge, read out the five further 'Quiet Zone' words to spell: **alert**, **nerve**, **mother**, **flower**, **brother**.

Full details of how to carry out assessment can be found on pages 6 and 108 of this guide.

STATION – WEEK 16

Girls Surf

OBJECTIVES
PART 1 – ir

Spell and use words in writing containing ir

Review previous learning

Ask the children if they can recall the spelling rule or any example words from the previous spelling lesson. Elicit ideas and remind the children that: In some words the spelling pattern **er** sounds like /er/. For example, **herb**. This is a stressed syllable. In other words the er spelling pattern is unstressed. It sounds like /u/. For example, **sister**.

Introducing the rule

Explain to the children that in today's lesson they will learn about words that are spelt with **ir**.

The /er/ sound can be spelt in many different ways. For example, **er** as in **herb**, **ir** as in **girl** and **ur** as in **turn**.

Optional: Review the Letterland character stories

Character-based stories can help children to remember spelling patterns (see page 123).

Pupil Book Activity 1: Picture Match

1. Draw children's attention to the Word Bank at the top of page 32. Explain that all of these words contain **ir**.
2. Ask the children to read through the words in the Word Bank and talk to a partner about what they mean. Then ask the children if there are any words they are unsure of and explain the meanings to them, looking in the dictionary for a definition if necessary.
3. Ask the children to find and copy words from the Word Bank to match the pictures.

Answers: a) bird; b) circle; c) skirt; d) girl; e) first; f) stir

Pupil Book Activity 2: Underline ir

1. Model the activity by choosing a word from the Word Bank and writing it on the board, for example: **girl**. Then underline the **ir** part of the word: **girl**
2. Ask the children to underline the **ir** spelling pattern in all of the words in the Word Bank.

Pupil Book Activity 3: Complete the Sentences

1. Read sentences **a** – **e** to the children, pausing as you reach each gap. Complete the first sentence with the children by re-reading to the first gap and then say: *Look at the Word Bank. Which word is something a dad might iron to get ready for work?* Elicit children's ideas and establish that the word is **shirt**.
2. Ask the children to fill in the gaps in the rest of the sentences independently or with a partner.

Answers: a) shirt; b) bird; c) stir; d) circle; e) dirty

Pupil Book Activity 4: Challenge!

1. Set the children the challenge of writing their own short story using **ir** words. Explain to the children that using the words in this way will help them to remember the words more effectively. Encourage the children to include as many of the Word Bank words as possible.

2. Use the following text as a model to show the children how to write the short story or, alternatively, use the text as a passage dictation by reading each sentence slowly and clearly for the children to write down:

A **girl** saw a **bird** as she walked down the path. It was the **first** time she had been this way. She could hear the bird **chirp** as she passed its nest. She wasn't looking and she tripped. Her **shirt** and **skirt** were both **dirty**.

Review previous learning

Ask the children if they can recall the spelling rule or any example words from the previous spelling lesson. Elicit ideas and remind the children that: The /er/ sound can be spelt in many different ways. For example, **er** as in **herb**, **ir** as in **girl** and **ur** as in **turn**.

OBJECTIVES
PART 2 – ur
Spell and use words in writing containing ur

Introducing the rule

Explain to the children that in today's lesson they will learn about words that are spelt with **ur**.

Optional: Review the Letterland character stories

Character-based stories can help children to remember spelling patterns (see page 123).

Pupil Book Activity 1: Picture Match

1. Draw the children's attention to the Word Bank at the top of page 33. Explain that all of these words contain **ur**.
2. Ask the children to read through the words in the Word Bank and talk to a partner about what they mean. Then ask the children if there are any words they are unsure of and explain the meanings to them, looking in the dictionary for a definition if necessary.
3. Ask the children to find and copy words from the Word Bank to match the pictures.

Answers: a) burger; b) turtle; c) purple

Pupil Book Activity 2: Word Match

1. Draw the children's attention to the words written underneath the blank drawing boxes.
2. Ask the children to read each word and talk to a partner about what they mean.
3. Ask the children to draw a simple picture to match the words underneath each box, for example, to match the word 'burst', children could draw bubbles or a balloon bursting.

Pupil Book Activity 3: Complete the Sentences

1. Read sentences **a – e** to the children, pausing as you reach each gap. Complete the first sentence with the children by re-reading to the first gap and then say: Look at the Word Bank. Which word is something you might do at a junction or crossroad in a car? Elicit the children's ideas and establish that the word is **turn**.
2. Ask the children to fill in the gaps in the rest of the sentences independently or with a partner.

Answers: a) turn; b) hurt; c) Thursday; d) burn; e) turtle

Pupil Book Activity 4: Challenge!

1. Draw the children's attention to the Word Search at the bottom of page 33. Set children the challenge of finding ten **ir** and **ur** words in the Word Search. Eight of the words run horizontally from left to right and two words run vertically from top to bottom.
2. Tell the children to circle each word as they find it and then write the words in two columns.

Answers:

f	a	n	g	b	i	r	d
i	b	u	r	g	e	r	h
r	l	s	h	i	r	t	u
s	b	b	u	r	s	t	r
t	g	i	r	l	c	f	t
d	k	t	h	i	r	d	h
T	h	u	r	s	d	a	y
e	m	j	t	u	r	n	i

ir	ur
fir	burger
bird	hurt
shirt	burst
girl	Thursday
third	turn

Assessment: ir, ur

Tell the children that you are going to read out ten words, one at a time. Each word will be one of the **ir** or **ur** words that they have been learning. Tell the children that you will say the word, and then you will read out a sentence containing the word to help them know what it means. You will then repeat the word on its own before pausing so that the children can write the word down. For example:
1. **girl**. There is a new **girl** in our class. **girl**

1. **girl**. There is a new **girl** in our class. **girl**
2. **turn**. I wait to have my **turn**. **turn**
3. **hurt**. We must not **hurt** others. **hurt**
4. **bird**. I saw a large **bird** in the sky. **bird**
5. **shirt**. I lost a button from my **shirt**. **shirt**
6. **burger**. I like ketchup on my **burger**. **burger**
7. **first**. I hope I get **first** place in the race. **first**
8. **burst**. My brother's balloon **burst**. **burst**
9. **third**. I was **third** in the line. **third**
10. **Thursday**. My favourite day of the week is **Thursday**. **Thursday**

For those students who need a bit more of a spelling challenge, read out the five further 'Quiet Zone' words to spell: **birthday, circus, thirst, injured, surprise**.

Full details of how to carry out assessment can be found on pages 6 and 108 of this guide.

STATION - WEEK 17
Cool B**oo**k

**OBJECTIVES
PART 1 – OO**

Spell and use words in writing containing oo

Review previous learning

Ask the children if they can recall the spelling rule or any example words from the previous spelling lesson. Elicit ideas and remind the children that: The /er/ sound can be spelt in many different ways. For example, **er** as in **herb**, **ir** as in **girl** and **ur** as in **turn**.

Introducing the rule

Explain to the children that in today's lesson they will learn about words that are spelt with the letters **oo** for the long /oo/ sound.

The spelling pattern **oo** can have a long /oo/ sound as in **food**, or it can have a short /oo/ sound as in **book**.

> **Optional: Review the Letterland character stories**
>
> Character-based stories can help children to remember spelling patterns (see page 123).

Pupil Book Activity 1: Picture Match

1. Draw children's attention to the Word Bank at the top of page 34. Explain that all of these words contain **oo**.
2. Ask the children to read through the words in the Word Bank and talk to a partner about what they mean. Then ask the children if there are any words they are unsure of and explain the meanings to them, looking in the dictionary for a definition if necessary.
3. Ask the children to find and copy words from the Word Bank to match the pictures.

Answers: a) boots; b) moon; c) zoo; d) hoop; e) goose; f) spoon

Pupil Book Activity 2: Underline oo

1. Model the activity by choosing a word from the Word Bank and writing it on the board, for example: **food**. Then underline the **oo** part of the word: **food**.
2. Ask the children to underline the **oo** spelling pattern in all of the words in the Word Bank.

Pupil Book Activity 3: Complete the Sentences

1. Read sentences **a** – **e** to the children, pausing as you reach each gap. Complete the first sentence with the children by re-reading to the first gap and then say: Look at the Word Bank. Which word is something you can swim in? Elicit children's ideas and establish that the word is **pool**.
2. Ask the children to fill in the gaps in the rest of the sentences independently or with a partner.

Answers: a) pool; b) zoo; c) room; d) hoop; e) broom

Pupil Book Activity 4: Challenge!

1. Set the children the challenge of writing their own short story using **oo** words. Explain to the children that using the words in this way will help them to remember the words more effectively. Encourage the children to include as many of the Word Bank words as possible.

2. Use the following text as a model to show the children how to write the short story or, alternatively, use the text as a passage dictation by reading each sentence slowly and clearly for the children to write down:

We ate our **food** then later we went in the **pool**. We stayed up until we saw the **moon**. In the morning we went to a **zoo**. I swept the insect **room** with a **broom**. As we left, a **goose** tried to peck my **boots**. It was the best holiday ever.

Review previous learning

Ask the children if they can recall the spelling rule or any example words from the previous spelling lesson. Elicit ideas and remind the children that: The spelling pattern **oo** can have a long /oo/ sound as in **food**, or it can have a short /oo/ sound as in **book**.

OBJECTIVES
PART 2 - oo /short/
Spell and use words in writing containing **oo**

Introducing the rule

Explain to the children that in today's lesson they will learn about words that are spelt with the letters **oo** for the short /oo/ sound.

> **Optional:** Review the Letterland character stories
> Character-based stories can help children to remember spelling patterns (see page 123).

Pupil Book Activity 1: Picture Match

1. Draw the children's attention to the Word Bank at the top of page 35. Explain that all of these words contain **oo**.
2. Ask the children to read through the words in the Word Bank and talk to a partner about what they mean. Then ask the children if there are any words they are unsure of and explain the meanings to them, looking in the dictionary for a definition if necessary.
3. Ask the children to find and copy words from the Word Bank to match the pictures.

Answers: a) hood; b) wood; c) crook

Pupil Book Activity 2: Word Match

1. Draw the children's attention to the words written underneath the blank drawing boxes.
2. Ask the children to read each word and talk to a partner about what they mean.
3. Ask the children to draw a simple picture to match the words underneath each box, for example, to match the word 'cook', children could draw themselves helping to cook.

Pupil Book Activity 3: Complete the Sentences

1. Read sentences **a – e** to the children, pausing as you reach each gap. Complete the first sentence with the children by re-reading to the first gap and then say: Look at the Word Bank. Which word is something that gets chopped up ready for a fire? Elicit the children's ideas and establish that the word is **wood**.
2. Ask the children to fill in the gaps in the rest of the sentences independently or with a partner.

Answers: a) wood; b) book; c) shook; d) cook; e) foot

Pupil Book Activity 4: Challenge!

1. Draw the children's attention to the Word Search at the bottom of page 35. Set children the challenge of finding ten **oo** (long /oo/) and **oo** (short /oo/) words in the Word Search. Eight of the words run horizontally from left to right and two words run vertically from top to bottom.
2. Tell the children to circle each word as they find it and then write the words in two columns.

Answers:

f	a	h	e	m	o	o	n
o	n	b	o	o	k	m	w
o	i	v	t	o	o	k	d
d	f	o	o	t	g	x	p
c	u	w	o	o	d	y	o
z	o	o	l	s	j	r	o
s	p	o	o	n	p	b	l
k	f	t	g	o	o	d	q

long /**oo**/	short /**oo**/
moon	book
food	took
pool	foot
zoo	wood
spoon	good

Assessment: oo, oo

Tell the children that you are going to read out ten words, one at a time. Each word will be one of the **oo** (long /oo/) or **oo** (short /oo/) words that they have been learning. Tell the children that you will say the word, and then you will read out a sentence containing the word to help them know what it means. You will then repeat the word on its own before pausing so that the children can write the word down. For example: 1. **food**. We went shopping to get **food**. **food**

1. **food**. We went shopping to get **food**. **food**
2. **pool**. I love to swim in the **pool**. **pool**
3. **moon**. We saw a full **moon**. **moon**
4. **book**. I am going to read a new **book**. **book**
5. **took**. I **took** some cookies from the jar. **took**
6. **zoo**. I saw lions at the **zoo**. **zoo**
7. **foot**. I kick the ball with my left **foot**. **foot**
8. **wood**. The table is made from **wood**. **wood**
9. **spoon**. I ate my cereal using a **spoon**. **spoon**
10. **good**. The cake tastes **good**. **good**

For those students who need a bit more of a spelling challenge, read out the five further 'Quiet Zone' words to spell: **balloon**, **tooth**, **proof**, **mistook**, **stood**.

Full details of how to carry out assessment can be found on pages 6 and 108 of this guide.

STATION - WEEK 18

Toad Toes

OBJECTIVES
PART 1 – oa
Spell and use words in writing containing **oa**

Review previous learning

Ask the children if they can recall the spelling rule or any example words from the previous spelling lesson. Elicit ideas and remind the children that: The spelling pattern **oo** can have a long /oo/ sound as in **food**, or it can have a short /oo/ sound as in **book**.

Introducing the rule

Explain to the children that in today's lesson they will learn about words that are spelt with **oa**.

The long vowel sound /oa/ can be spelt in many different ways. For example, **oa** as in **coat**, **o_e** as in **rose** and **ow** as in **snow**.

Optional: Review the Letterland character stories

Character-based stories can help children to remember spelling patterns (see page 123).

Pupil Book Activity 1: Picture Match

1. Draw children's attention to the Word Bank at the top of page 36. Explain that all of these words contain **oa**.
2. Ask the children to read through the words in the Word Bank and talk to a partner about what they mean. Then ask the children if there are any words they are unsure of and explain the meanings to them, looking in the dictionary for a definition if necessary.
3. Ask the children to find and copy words from the Word Bank to match the pictures.

Answers: a) toad; b) goat; c) goal; d) boat; e) coach; f) coat

Pupil Book Activity 2: Underline oa

1. Model the activity by choosing a word from the Word Bank and writing it on the board, for example: **boat**. Then underline the **oa** part of the word: b**oa**t
2. Ask the children to underline the **oa** spelling pattern in all of the words in the Word Bank.

Pupil Book Activity 3: Complete the Sentences

1. Read sentences **a** – **e** to the children, pausing as you reach each gap. Complete the first sentence with the children by re-reading to the first gap and then say: Look at the Word Bank. Which word is something you can score to win? Elicit children's ideas and establish that the word is **goal**.
2. Ask the children to fill in the gaps in the rest of the sentences independently or with a partner.

Answers: a) goal; b) boat; c) soap; d) toad; e) float

Pupil Book Activity 4: Challenge!

1. Set the children the challenge of writing their own short story using oa words. Explain to the children that using the words in this way will help them to remember the words more effectively. Encourage the children to include as many of the Word Bank words as possible.
2. Use the following text as a model to show the children how to write the short story or, alternatively, use the text as a passage dictation by reading each sentence slowly and clearly for the children to

write down:

We put on our **coats** then we got on the **boat**. As the **boat** set sail we looked back at the **road** and saw the **coach**. 'Those people are too late to get onboard The Royal **Oak boat**,' I thought. A man pulling a **goat** on a rope ran towards the **boat** but he slipped on some **soap**. He landed next to a **toad** in the water. Luckily he could **float**.

> **OBJECTIVES**
> **PART 2 – oe**
> Spell and use words in writing containing **oe**

Review previous learning

Ask the children if they can recall the spelling rule or any example words from the previous spelling lesson. Elicit ideas and remind the children that: The long vowel sound /oa/ can be spelt in many different ways. For example, **oa** as in **coat**, **o_e** as in **rose** and **ow** as in **snow**.

Introducing the rule

Explain to the children that in today's lesson they will learn about words that are spelt with **oe**. Explain that this is another way of spelling the /oa/ sound but it is rare and there are not many examples. Show the Word Bank and explain that there are some words that are spelt with oe but only when there is more than one of that item (plural). Emphasise that in the singular, these words end in **o** and not **oe**.

> **Optional: Letterland character stories**
>
> The simple rule is, 'When two Vowel Men go out walking, the first man does the talking'. There is no particular artwork to show this spelling pattern as it is so rarely used.

Pupil Book Activity 1: Picture Match

1. Draw the children's attention to the Word Bank at the top of page 37. Explain that all of these words contain **oe**.
2. Ask the children to read through the words in the Word Bank and talk to a partner about what they mean. Then ask the children if there are any words they are unsure of and explain the meanings to them, looking in the dictionary for a definition if necessary.
3. Ask the children to find and copy words from the Word Bank to match the pictures.

Answers: a) doe; b) oboe; c) aloe

Pupil Book Activity 2: Word Match

1. Draw the children's attention to the words written underneath the blank drawing boxes.
2. Ask the children to read each word and talk to a partner about what they mean.
3. Ask the children to draw a simple picture to match the words underneath each box, for example, to match the word 'tomatoes', children could draw a vine of tomatoes. Remind the children that they must draw more than one for the plurals.

Pupil Book Activity 3: Complete the Sentences

1. Read sentences **a** – **e** to the children, pausing as you reach each gap. Complete the first sentence with the children by re-reading to the first gap and then say: Look at the Word Bank. Which word is something that can erupt? Elicit the children's ideas and establish that the word is **volcanoes**.
2. Ask the children to fill the gaps in the rest of the sentences independently or with a partner.

Answers: a) volcanoes; b) potatoes; c) doe; d) oboe; e) toe

Pupil Book Activity 4: Challenge!

1. Draw the children's attention to the Word Search at the bottom of page 37. Set children the challenge of finding ten **oa** and **oe** words in the Word Search. Eight of the words run horizontally from left to right and two words run vertically from top to bottom.
2. Tell the children to circle each word as they find it and then write the words in two columns.

Answers:

w	h	p	o	b	o	e	l
o	b	o	a	t	i	q	b
e	c	g	c	o	a	t	m
o	r	o	a	d	j	n	t
d	f	c	o	a	c	h	o
g	o	a	l	e	t	r	e
h	e	r	o	e	s	k	a
t	o	m	a	t	o	e	s

oa	oe
boat	woe
coat	toe
road	oboe
coach	heroes
goal	tomatoes

Assessment: oa, oe

Tell the children that you are going to read out ten words, one at a time. Each word will be one of the **oa** or **oe** words that they have been learning. Tell the children that you will say the word, and then you will read out a sentence containing the word to help them know what it means. You will then repeat the word on its own before pausing so that the children can write the word down. For example:
1. **boat**. We went fishing on the **boat**. **boat**

1. **boat**. We went fishing on the **boat**. **boat**
2. **toe**. I have a cut on my big **toe**. **toe**
3. **coat**. I wear my **coat** when it is cold. **coat**
4. **doe**. The **doe** looked after its baby. **doe**
5. **road**. I saw a motorbike on the **road**. **road**
6. **oboe**. My sister is learning to play the **oboe**. **oboe**
7. **coach**. We are going on a **coach** on our school trip. **coach**
8. **aloe**. My mum put **aloe** vera plants in our garden. **aloe**
9. **goal**. Tommy scored a **goal**. **goal**
10. **woe**. I felt **woe** when my cat was lost. **woe**

For those students who need a bit more of a spelling challenge, read out the five further 'Quiet Zone' words to spell: **throat**, **coast**, **potatoes**, **tomatoes**, **volcanoes**.

Full details of how to carry out assessment can be found on pages 6 and 108 of this guide.

STATION - WEEK 19
Snow House

OBJECTIVES
PART 1 – ow

Spell and use words in writing containing **ow**

Review previous learning

Ask the children if they can recall the spelling rule or any example words from the previous spelling lesson. Elicit ideas and remind the children that: The long vowel sound /oa/ can be spelt in many different ways. For example, **oa** as in **coat**, **o_e** as in **rose** and **ow** as in **snow**. It can also be spelt as **oe** as in **toe** but this is rare.

Introducing the rule

Explain to the children that in today's lesson they will learn about words that are spelt with the letters **ow** for the /oa/ sound.

The long vowel sound /oa/ can be spelt in many different ways. For example, **oa** as in **coat**, **o_e** as in **rose** and **ow** as in **snow**.

Optional: Review the Letterland character stories

Character-based stories can help children to remember spelling patterns (see page 123).

Pupil Book Activity 1: Picture Match

1. Draw children's attention to the Word Bank at the top of page 38. Explain that all of these words contain **ow**.
2. Ask the children to read through the words in the Word Bank and talk to a partner about what they mean. Then ask the children if there are any words they are unsure of and explain the meanings to them, looking in the dictionary for a definition if necessary.
3. Ask the children to find and copy words from the Word Bank to match the pictures.

Answers: a) snow; b) elbow; c) throw; d) arrow; e) grow; f) blow

Pupil Book Activity 2: Underline ow

1. Model the activity by choosing a word from the Word Bank and writing it on the board, for example: **own**. Then underline the **ow** part of the word: **own**
2. Ask the children to underline the ow spelling pattern in all of the words in the Word Bank.

Pupil Book Activity 3: Complete the Sentences

1. Read sentences **a – e** to the children, pausing as you reach each gap. Complete the first sentence with the children by re-reading to the first gap and then say: Look at the Word Bank. Which word is something that you can watch? Elicit children's ideas and establish that the word is **show**.
2. Ask the children to fill in the gaps in the rest of the sentences independently or with a partner.

Answers: a) show; b) snow; c) grow; d) slow; e) throw

Pupil Book Activity 4: Challenge!

1. Set the children the challenge of writing their own short story using **ow** words. Explain to the children that using the words in this way will help them to remember the words more effectively. Encourage the children to include as many of the Word Bank words as possible.

2. Use the following text as a model to show the children how to write the short story or, alternatively, use the text as a passage dictation by reading each sentence slowly and clearly for the children to write down:

Dan plays in the **snow**. He can **blow** the **snow** off his glove. He can lay **low** in the **snow** and wiggle his **elbow** to make a pattern. He can **throw snowballs** at the gate. He can **show** his mum the **snowman** he has made.

Watch Out!

Draw children's attention to the Watch Out! box at the bottom of page 38. Explain to the children that the **ow** spelling pattern can also have an /ou/ sound as in **brown**, covered in Week 20.

Review previous learning

Ask the children if they can recall the spelling rule or any example words from the previous spelling lesson. Elicit ideas and remind the children that: The long vowel sound /oa/ can be spelt in many different ways. For example, **oa** as in **coat**, **o_e** as in **rose** and **ow** as in **snow**.

> **OBJECTIVES**
> **PART 2 – Tricky Words**
> Spell and use tricky words in writing

Introducing the rule

Explain to the children that in today's lesson they will learn about words that can be difficult to spell because the letter-sound correspondences in them have not yet been taught, but the words are so useful that we want to use them now.

Some words do not sound the way you might expect them to. Pay attention to which parts of the word you know and which parts are tricky.

Pupil Book Activity 1: Read the Word Bank and Example Sentences

1. Draw the children's attention to the Word Bank in the left-hand column of page 39. Explain that all of these words contain parts that have not yet been taught but that it is likely the children will know how to read the words from encountering them in reading books.
2. Ask the children to read through the words in the Word Bank and talk to a partner about what they mean. Then ask the children if there are any words they are unsure of and explain the meanings to them, looking in the dictionary for a definition if necessary.
3. Ask the children to read the example sentences in the second column to help them understand the words in context.

Pupil Book Activity 2: Colour the Parts

1. Draw the children's attention to the third column which contains the words shown so that each phoneme (sound) is distinguishable.
2. Ask the children to say the sounds while thinking carefully about the whole word. Remind them that the letters may not sound the way they expect.
3. Ask the children to colour the easy parts of the words in green and the tricky parts in orange. For example in the word 'there' the 'th' letters represent the /th/ sound but the 'ere' letters represent an /air/ sound. Alternatively, ask them to draw a wiggly line under the tricky parts.

Pupil Book Activity 3: Write the Word

1. In the final column ask the children to write each word. If they feel confident they could cover up the information in the other columns. If they lack confidence they should copy the spelling from the other

columns and say the word as they write it.

2. Remind the children to look back through their spellings to check for accuracy.

Assessment: ow, Tricky Words

Tell the children that you are going to read out ten words, one at a time. Each word will be one of the **ow** or tricky words that they have been learning. Tell the children that you will say the word, and then you will read out a sentence containing the word to help them know what it means. You will then repeat the word on its own before pausing so that the children can write the word down. For example: 1. **own**. I **own** two pairs of shoes. **own**

1. **own**. I **own** two pairs of shoes. **own**
2. **blow**. I **blow** the candles out on my cake. **blow**
3. **here**. I have been **here** before. **here**
4. **there**. We went **there** yesterday. **there**
5. **snow**. I like to play in the **snow**. **snow**
6. **grow**. I like to **grow** vegetables. **grow**
7. **where**. I know **where** the books are kept. **where**
8. **come**. Can you **come** to my house for tea? **come**
9. **arrow**. I drew an **arrow** to show which way to go. **arrow**
10. **one**. I have **one** older sister. **one**

For those students who need a bit more of a spelling challenge, read out the five further 'Quiet Zone' words to spell: **below**, **rainbow**, **pillow**, **friend**, **house**.

Full details of how to carry out assessment can be found on pages 6 and 108 of this guide.

Station – Week 20: Loud Town

OBJECTIVES

PART 1 – ou

Spell and use words in writing containing ou

Review previous learning

Ask the children if they can recall the spelling rule or any example words from the previous spelling lesson. Elicit ideas and remind the children that: Some words do not sound the way you might expect them to. Pay attention to which parts of the word you know and which parts are tricky.

Introducing the rule

Explain to the children that in today's lesson they will learn about words that are spelt with **ou**.

The /ou/ sound can be spelt in different ways. For example, **ou** as in **out** and **ow** as in **now**.

Optional: Review the Letterland character stories

Character-based stories can help children to remember spelling patterns (see page 123).

Pupil Book Activity 1: Picture Match

1. Draw children's attention to the Word Bank at the top of page 40. Explain that all of these words contain **ou**.
2. Ask the children to read through the words in the Word Bank and talk to a partner about what they mean. Then ask the children if there are any words they are unsure of and explain the meanings to them, looking in the dictionary for a definition if necessary.
3. Ask the children to find and copy words from the Word Bank to match the pictures.

Answers: a) mouth; b) cloud; c) pouch; d) mouse; e) shout; f) count

Pupil Book Activity 2: Underline ou

1. Model the activity by choosing a word from the Word Bank and writing it on the board, for example: **out**. Then underline the **ou** part of the word: **out**.
2. Ask the children to underline the **ou** spelling pattern in all of the words in the Word Bank.

Pupil Book Activity 3: Complete the Sentences

1. Read sentences **a – e** to the children, pausing as you reach each gap. Complete the first sentence with the children by re-reading to the first gap and then say: Look at the Word Bank. Which word is something that you can do to one hundred? Elicit children's ideas and establish that the word is **count**.
2. Ask the children to fill in the gaps in the rest of the sentences independently or with a partner.

Answers: a) count; b) out; c) mouth; d) cloud; e) mouse

Pupil Book Activity 4: Challenge!

1. Set the children the challenge of writing their own short story using **ou** words. Explain to the children that using the words in this way will help them to remember the words more effectively. Encourage the children to include as many of the Word Bank words as possible.
2. Use the following text as a model to show the children how to write the short story or, alternatively,

use the text as a passage dictation by reading each sentence slowly and clearly for the children to write down:

Imran opened his **mouth** to shout when he saw the **mouse**. "I was about to **count** the money in my **pouch** when I saw it," he said. He opened the door and it ran **out** without making a **sound**.

Watch Out!

1. Draw children's attention to the Watch Out! box at the bottom of page 40. Explain to the children that the letters **ou** don't always represent an /ou/ sound. For example, **should**, **could** and **would**. In these words the **ou** letters work with the **l** (oul) to represent a short /oo/ sound.

Review previous learning

Ask the children if they can recall the spelling rule or any example words from the previous spelling lesson. Elicit ideas and remind the children that: The /ou/ sound can be spelt in different ways. For example, **ou** as in **out** and **ow** as in **now**.

> **OBJECTIVES**
> **PART 2 – ow**
>
> **Spell and use words in writing containing ow**

Introducing the rule

Explain to the children that in today's lesson they will learn about words that are spelt with **ow**.

The /ou/ sound can be spelt in different ways. For example, **ou** as in **out** and **ow** as in **now**.

Optional: Review the Letterland character stories
Character-based stories can help children to remember spelling patterns (see page 123).

Pupil Book Activity 1: Picture Match

1. Draw the children's attention to the Word Bank at the top of page 41. Explain that all of these words contain **ow**.
2. Ask the children to read through the words in the Word Bank and talk to a partner about what they mean. Then ask the children if there are any words they are unsure of and explain the meanings to them, looking in the dictionary for a definition if necessary.
3. Ask the children to find and copy words from the Word Bank to match the pictures.

Answers: a) towel; b) owl; c) cow

Pupil Book Activity 2: Word Match

1. Draw the children's attention to the words written underneath the blank drawing boxes.
2. Ask the children to read each word and talk to a partner about what they mean.
3. Ask the children to draw a simple picture to match the words underneath each box, for example, to match the word 'frown', children could draw themselves with a frowning expression.

Pupil Book Activity 3: Complete the Sentences

1. Read sentences **a – e** to the children, pausing as you reach each gap. Complete the first sentence with the children by re-reading to the first gap and then say: Look at the Word Bank. Which word is something that a Queen might wear? Elicit the children's ideas and establish that the word is **crown**. An alternative acceptable answer is **gown**.

2. Ask the children to fill in the gaps in the rest of the sentences independently or with a partner.
Answers: a) crown/gown; b) town; c) growl; d) frown; e) cow

Pupil Book Activity 4: Challenge!

1. Draw the children's attention to the Word Search at the bottom of page 41. Set children the challenge of finding ten **ou** and **ow** words in the Word Search. Eight of the words run horizontally from left to right and two words run vertically from top to bottom.
2. Tell the children to circle each word as they find it and then write the words in two columns.

Answers:

c	r	o	w	n	f	s	q
t	e	d	o	u	t	o	n
o	a	b	o	u	t	p	f
w	c	g	o	w	n	m	r
e	h	m	o	u	t	h	o
l	a	r	o	u	n	d	w
s	o	u	n	d	i	j	n
b	g	o	w	l	k	a	l

ou	ow
out	towel
about	crown
mouth	gown
around	frown
sound	owl

Assessment: ou, ow

Tell the children that you are going to read out ten words, one at a time. Each word will be one of the **ou** or **ow** words that they have been learning. Tell the children that you will say the word, and then you will read out a sentence containing the word to help them know what it means. You will then repeat the word on its own before pausing so that the children can write the word down. For example: 1. **out**. I took the ball **out** of the shed. **out**

1. **out**. I took the ball **out** of the shed. **out**
2. **crown**. The **crown** was covered in jewels. **crown**
3. **about**. I learned **about** the planets. **about**
4. **mouth**. An alligator has a large **mouth**. **mouth**
5. **towel**. I took a **towel** to the beach. **towel**
6. **around**. We walked **around** the forest. **around**
7. **sound**. My trumpet makes a loud **sound**. **sound**
8. **frown**. My gran has a **frown** when she thinks hard. **frown**
9. **owl**. I heard an **owl** in the night. **owl**
10. **gown**. The princess wore a glittering **gown**. **gown**

For those students who need a bit more of a spelling challenge, read out the five further 'Quiet Zone' words to spell: **pound, flour, brow, scowl, howl**.

Full details of how to carry out assessment can be found on pages 6 and 108 of this guide.

STATION - WEEK 21
Blue Crew

OBJECTIVES
PART 1 – ue
Spell and use words in writing containing ue

Review previous learning
Ask the children if they can recall the spelling rule or any example words from the previous spelling lesson. Elicit ideas and remind the children that: The /ou/ sound can be spelt in different ways. For example, **ou** as in **out** and **ow** as in **now**.

Introducing the rule
Explain to the children that in today's lesson they will learn about words that are spelt with **ue** when it represents a long /oo/ sound as in **blue**.

Both the /oo/ and the /yoo/ sounds can be spelt as **u_e**, **ue** and **ew**. If words end in the /oo/ sound, **ue** and **ew** are more common spellings than **oo**.

Optional: Review the Letterland character stories
Character-based stories can help children to remember spelling patterns (see page 123).

Pupil Book Activity 1: Picture Match
1. Draw children's attention to the Word Bank at the top of page 42. Explain that all of these words contain **ue** when it represents a long /oo/ sound.
2. Ask the children to read through the words in the Word Bank and talk to a partner about what they mean. Then ask the children if there are any words they are unsure of and explain the meanings to them, looking in the dictionary for a definition if necessary.
3. Ask the children to find and copy words from the Word Bank to match the pictures.

Answers: a) tissue; b) Sue; c) glue; d) clue; e) true; f) blue

Pupil Book Activity 2: Underline ue
1. Model the activity by choosing a word from the Word Bank and writing it on the board, for example: **blue**. Then underline the **ue** part of the word: **bl<u>ue</u>**.
2. Ask the children to underline the **ue** spelling pattern in all of the words in the Word Bank.

Pupil Book Activity 3: Complete the Sentences
1. Read sentences **a – e** to the children, pausing as you reach each gap. Complete the first sentence with the children by re-reading to the first gap and then say: Look at the Word Bank. Which word is something that you can use to stick things with? Elicit children's ideas and establish that the word is **glue**.
2. Ask the children to fill in the gaps in the rest of the sentences independently or with a partner.

Answers: a) glue; b) cruel; c) tissue; d) blue; e) Sue

Pupil Book Activity 4: Challenge!
1. Set the children the challenge of writing their own short story using **ue** words. Explain to the children that using the words in this way will help them to remember the words more effectively. Encourage

the children to include as many of the Word Bank words as possible.

2. Use the following text as a model to show the children how to write the short story or, alternatively, use the text as a passage dictation by reading each sentence slowly and clearly for the children to write down:

I used a **blue** pen to write the **clue**. It is **true** that I used **glue** to stick it on the desk. My teacher was **cruel** and said I must scrub off the **glue** with a **tissue**. The **issue** was we had run out of **tissues**.

Watch Out!

Draw children's attention to the Watch Out! box at the bottom of page 42. Explain to the children that the spelling pattern **ue** can represent an /oo/ sound or it can represent a /yoo/ sound.

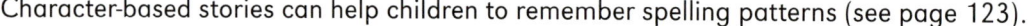

Review previous learning

Ask the children if they can recall the spelling rule or any example words from the previous spelling lesson. Elicit ideas and remind the children that: Both the /oo/ and the /yoo/ sounds can be spelt as **u_e**, **ue** and **ew**. If words end in the /oo/ sound, **ue** and **ew** are more common spellings than **oo**.

**OBJECTIVES
PART 2 – ew

Spell and use words in writing containing ew**

Introducing the rule

Explain to the children that in today's lesson they will learn about words that are spelt with **ew** when it represents a long /oo/ sound as in **grew**.

Both the /oo/ and the /yoo/ sounds can be spelt as **u_e**, **ue** and **ew**. If words end in the /oo/ sound, **ue** and **ew** are more common spellings than **oo**.

Optional: Review the Letterland character stories

Character-based stories can help children to remember spelling patterns (see page 123).

Pupil Book Activity 1: Picture Match

1. Draw the children's attention to the Word Bank at the top of page 43. Explain that all of these words contain **ew**.
2. Ask the children to read through the words in the Word Bank and talk to a partner about what they mean. Then ask the children if there are any words they are unsure of and explain the meanings to them, looking in the dictionary for a definition if necessary.
3. Ask the children to find and copy words from the Word Bank to match the pictures.

Answers: a) shrew; b) grew; c) drew

Pupil Book Activity 2: Word Match

1. Draw the children's attention to the words written underneath the blank drawing boxes.
2. Ask the children to read each word and talk to a partner about what they mean.
3. Ask the children to draw a simple picture to match the words underneath each box, for example, to match the word 'brew', children could draw a person brewing a pot of tea.

Pupil Book Activity 3: Complete the Sentences

1. Read sentences **a – e** to the children, pausing as you reach each gap. Complete the first sentence with the children by re-reading to the first gap and then say: Look at the Word Bank. Which word

is something that might result in a picture? Elicit the children's ideas and establish that the word is **drew**.

2. Ask the children to fill in the gaps in the rest of the sentences independently or with a partner.

Answers: a) drew; b) grew; c) chew; d) flew; e) threw

Pupil Book Activity 4: Challenge!

1. Draw the children's attention to the Word Search at the bottom of page 43. Set children the challenge of finding ten **ue** and **ew** words in the Word Search. Eight of the words run horizontally from left to right and two words run vertically from top to bottom.
2. Tell the children to circle each word as they find it and then write the words in two columns.

Answers:

c	t	r	u	e	i	r	c
g	r	e	w	b	j	p	l
a	h	q	f	l	e	w	u
b	o	g	l	u	e	s	e
l	d	r	e	w	t	y	n
u	g	t	h	r	e	w	k
e	m	t	i	s	s	u	e
d	c	h	e	w	f	e	l

ue	ew
true	grew
blue	flew
clue	drew
glue	threw
tissue	chew

Watch Out!

Draw children's attention to the Watch Out! box at the bottom of page 43. Explain to the children that the spelling pattern **ew** can represent an /oo/ sound or it can represent a /yoo/ sound.

Assessment: ue, ew

Tell the children that you are going to read out ten words, one at a time. Each word will be one of the **ue** or **ew** words that they have been learning. Tell the children that you will say the word, and then you will read out a sentence containing the word to help them know what it means. You will then repeat the word on its own before pausing so that the children can write the word down. For example: 1. **blue**. I like to write in a **blue** pen. **blue**

3. **blue**. I like to write in a **blue** pen. **blue**
4. **grew**. The flowers **grew** taller than the fence. **grew**
5. **clue**. I followed the **clue** to find the prize. **clue**
6. **true**. Our teacher told us a **true** story. **true**
7. **flew**. The birds **flew** South for the winter. **flew**
8. **drew**. We **drew** pictures of the forest. **drew**
9. **glue**. I stuck my picture with **glue**. **glue**
10. **threw**. My gran **threw** the ball at the wall. **threw**
11. **chew**. I like sweets that you can **chew**. **chew**
12. **cruel**. The villain in the story is often **cruel**. **cruel**

For those students who need a bit more of a spelling challenge, read out the five further 'Quiet Zone' words to spell: **gruesome**, **clueless**, **screws**, **jewels**, **cashew**.

STATION - WEEK 22
New Statue

OBJECTIVES
PART 1 – ew

Spell and use words in writing containing **ew**

Review previous learning

Ask the children if they can recall the spelling rule or any example words from the previous spelling lesson. Elicit ideas and remind the children that: Both the /oo/ and the /yoo/ sounds can be spelt as **u_e**, **ue** and **ew**. If words end in the /oo/ sound, **ue** and **ew** are more common spellings than **oo**.

Introducing the rule

Explain to the children that in today's lesson they will learn about words that are spelt with **ew** when it represents a /yoo/ sound as in **new**.

> **Optional: Review the Letterland character stories**
> Character-based stories can help children to remember spelling patterns (see page 123).

Pupil Book Activity 1: Picture Match

1. Draw children's attention to the Word Bank at the top of page 44. Explain that all of these words contain **ew**.
2. Ask the children to read through the words in the Word Bank and talk to a partner about what they mean. Then ask the children if there are any words they are unsure of and explain the meanings to them, looking in the dictionary for a definition if necessary.
3. Ask the children to find and copy words from the Word Bank to match the pictures.

Answers: a) ewe; b) news; c) newborn; d) stew; e) nephew; f) new

Pupil Book Activity 2: Underline ew

1. Model the activity by choosing a word from the Word Bank and writing it on the board, for example: **new**. Then underline the **ew** part of the word: n**ew**.
2. Ask the children to underline the **ew** spelling pattern in all of the words in the Word Bank.

Pupil Book Activity 3: Complete the Sentences

1. Read sentences **a – e** to the children, pausing as you reach each gap. Complete the first sentence with the children by re-reading to the first gap and then say: *Look at the Word Bank. Which word is something that you could watch everyday?* Elicit children's ideas and establish that the word is the **news**.
2. Ask the children to fill in the gaps in the rest of the sentences independently or with a partner.

Answers: a) news; b) few; c) knew; d) stew; e) ewe

Pupil Book Activity 4: Challenge!

1. Set the children the challenge of writing their own short story using **ew** words. Explain to the children that using the words in this way will help them to remember the words more effectively. Encourage the children to include as many of the Word Bank words as possible.
2. Use the following text as a model to show the children how to write the short story or, alternatively, use the text as a passage dictation by reading each sentence slowly and clearly for the children to

write down:

Sara **knew** it was only a **few** days until he would get to meet her **newborn nephew**. When **news** had arrived that he had been born she went shopping to buy him a **few** gifts. One of the gifts was a cuddly toy **ewe**.

Watch Out!

Draw children's attention to the Watch Out! box at the bottom of page 44. Explain to the children that the spelling pattern **ew** can represent an /oo/ sound or it can represent a /yoo/ sound.

Review previous learning

Ask the children if they can recall the spelling rule or any example words from the previous spelling lesson. Elicit ideas and remind the children that: Both the /oo/ and the /yoo/ sounds can be spelt as **u_e**, **ue** and **ew**. If words end in the /oo/ sound, **ue** and **ew** are more common spellings than **oo**.

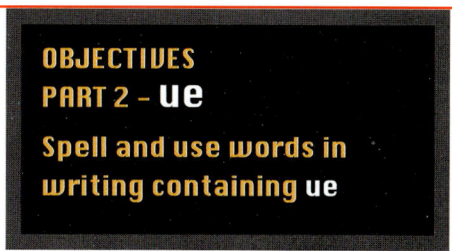

**OBJECTIVES
PART 2 – ue
Spell and use words in writing containing ue**

Introducing the rule

Explain to the children that in today's lesson they will learn about words that are spelt with **ue** when it represents a /yoo/ sound as in **rescue**.

Optional: Review the Letterland character stories

Character-based stories can help children to remember spelling patterns (see page 123).

Pupil Book Activity 1: Picture Match

1. Draw the children's attention to the Word Bank at the top of page 45. Explain that all of these words contain **ue**.
2. Ask the children to read through the words in the Word Bank and talk to a partner about what they mean. Then ask the children if there are any words they are unsure of and explain the meanings to them, looking in the dictionary for a definition if necessary.
3. Ask the children to find and copy words from the Word Bank to match the pictures.

Answers: a) barbecue; b) queue; c) argue

Pupil Book Activity 2: Word Match

1. Draw the children's attention to the words written underneath the blank drawing boxes.
2. Ask the children to read each word and talk to a partner about what they mean.
3. Ask the children to draw a simple picture to match the words underneath each box, for example, to match the word 'rescue', children could draw an exciting mountain or sea rescue happening.

Pupil Book Activity 3: Complete the Sentences

1. Read sentences **a – e** to the children, pausing as you reach each gap. Complete the first sentence with the children by re-reading to the first gap and then say: Look at the Word Bank. Which word is a day of the week? Elicit the children's ideas and establish that the word is **Tuesday**.
2. Ask the children to fill in the gaps in the rest of the sentences independently or with a partner.

Answers: a) Tuesday; b) queue; c) fuel; d) argue; e) statue

Pupil Book Activity 4: Challenge!

1. Draw the children's attention to the Word Search at the bottom of page 45. Set children the challenge of finding ten **ew** and **ue** words in the Word Search. Eight of the words run horizontally from left to right and two words run vertically from top to bottom.
2. Tell the children to circle each word as they find it and then write the words in two columns.

Answers:

k	n	e	w	c	g	q	f
a	r	g	u	e	j	n	e
b	f	v	a	l	u	e	w
k	n	e	p	h	e	w	h
p	e	f	u	e	l	d	r
n	s	t	a	t	u	e	l
e	i	r	e	s	c	u	e
w	o	a	s	t	e	w	m

ue	ew
argue	knew
value	few
fuel	new
statue	stew
rescue	nephew

Watch Out!

Draw children's attention to the Watch Out! box on page 45. Explain to the children that the spelling pattern **ue** can represent an /oo/ sound or it can represent a /yoo/ sound.

Assessment: ew, ue

Tell the children that you are going to read out ten words, one at a time. Each word will be one of the **ew** or **ue** words that they have been learning. Tell the children that you will say the word, and then you will read out a sentence containing the word to help them know what it means. You will then repeat the word on its own before pausing so that the children can write the word down. For example: 1. **new**. I got a **new** scooter. **new**

3. **new**. I got a **new** scooter. **new**
4. **few**. There were only a **few** bananas left. **few**
5. **knew**. I **knew** all about the frog in the pond. **knew**
6. **rescue**. A man has gone to **rescue** the kitten. **rescue**
7. **Tuesday**. I am going to the park on **Tuesday**. **Tuesday**
8. **argue**. We heard the women **argue**. **argue**
9. **stew**. My dinner was **stew**. **stew**
10. **barbecue**. My dad set up the **barbecue**. **barbecue**
11. **queue**. I waited in a **queue** to go on the ride. **queue**
12. **nephew**. My **nephew** is just a baby. **nephew**

For those students who need a bit more of a spelling challenge, read out the five further 'Quiet Zone' words to spell: **skewer, mildew, value, statue, overdue**.

STATION - WEEK 23
Tie Bright

OBJECTIVES
PART 1 – ie

Spell and use words in writing containing **ie**

Review previous learning

Ask the children if they can recall the spelling rule or any example words from the previous spelling lesson. Elicit ideas and remind the children that: Both the /oo/ and the /yoo/ sounds can be spelt as **u_e**, **ue** and **ew**. If words end in the /oo/ sound, **ue** and **ew** are more common spellings than **oo**.

Introducing the rule

Explain to the children that in today's lesson they will learn about words that are spelt with **ie**.

The long vowel sound /igh/ can be spelt in many different ways. For example, **ie** as in **tie**, **igh** as in **night**, **i_e** as in **bike** and **y** as in **cry**.

> **Optional: Review the Letterland character stories**
>
> Character-based stories can help children to remember spelling patterns (see page 123).

Pupil Book Activity 1: Picture Match

1. Draw children's attention to the Word Bank at the top of page 46. Explain that all of these words contain **ie**.
2. Ask the children to read through the words in the Word Bank and talk to a partner about what they mean. Then ask the children if there are any words they are unsure of and explain the meanings to them, looking in the dictionary for a definition if necessary.
3. Ask the children to find and copy words from the Word Bank to match the pictures.

Answers: a) magpie; b) pie; c) tie; d) fried; e) dried; f) necktie

Pupil Book Activity 2: Underline ie

1. Model the activity by choosing a word from the Word Bank and writing it on the board, for example: **lie**. Then underline the **ie** part of the word: l**ie**.
2. Ask the children to underline the **ie** spelling pattern in all of the words in the Word Bank.

Pupil Book Activity 3: Complete the Sentences

1. Read sentences **a – e** to the children, pausing as you reach each gap. Complete the first sentence with the children by re-reading to the first gap and then say: Look at the Word Bank. Which word is something associated with cooking? Elicit children's ideas and establish that the word is **fried**.
2. Ask the children to fill in the gaps in the rest of the sentences independently or with a partner.

Answers: a) fried; b) lie; c) cried; d) tried; e) dried

Pupil Book Activity 4: Challenge!

1. Set the children the challenge of writing their own short story using **ie** words. Explain to the children that using the words in this way will help them to remember the words more effectively. Encourage the children to include as many of the Word Bank words as possible.
2. Use the following text as a model to show the children how to write the short story or, alternatively,

use the text as a passage dictation by reading each sentence slowly and clearly for the children to write down:

Kevin **cried** when he told a **lie**. He **tried** the **pie** but didn't like it. It was **fried** and all **dried** up. He pretended to eat it but really he gave it to a **magpie**.

Watch Out!

Draw children's attention to the Watch Out! box at the bottom of page 46. Explain to the children that the **ie** spelling pattern can represent an /igh/ sound but in some words it can also be an /ee/ sound as in **piece** and **field**.

Review previous learning

Ask the children if they can recall the spelling rule or any example words from the previous spelling lesson. Elicit ideas and remind the children that: The long vowel sound /igh/ can be spelt in many different ways. For example, **ie** as in **tie**, **igh** as in **night**, **i_e** as in **bike** and **y** as in **cry**.

OBJECTIVES
PART 2 – igh
Spell and use words in writing containing igh

Introducing the rule

Explain to the children that in today's lesson they will learn about words that are spelt with **igh**.

Optional: Review the Letterland character stories

Character-based stories can help children to remember spelling patterns (see page 123).

Pupil Book Activity 1: Picture Match

1. Draw the children's attention to the Word Bank at the top of page 47. Explain that all of these words contain **igh**.
2. Ask the children to read through the words in the Word Bank and talk to a partner about what they mean. Then ask the children if there are any words they are unsure of and explain the meanings to them, looking in the dictionary for a definition if necessary.
3. Ask the children to find and copy words from the Word Bank to match the pictures.

Answers: a) night; b) right; c) flight

Pupil Book Activity 2: Word Match

1. Draw the children's attention to the words written underneath the blank drawing boxes.
2. Ask the children to read each word and talk to a partner about what they mean.
3. Ask the children to draw a simple picture to match the words underneath each box, for example, to match the word 'fright', children could draw themselves with a startled expression.

Pupil Book Activity 3: Complete the Sentences

1. Read sentences **a – e** to the children, pausing as you reach each gap. Complete the first sentence with the children by re-reading to the first gap and then say: Look at the Word Bank. Which word is something that a piece of clothing could become over time? Elicit the children's ideas and establish that the word is **tight**.

2. Ask the children to fill in the gaps in the rest of the sentences independently or with a partner.
Answers: a) tight; b) high; c) bright; d) right; e) knight

Pupil Book Activity 4: Challenge!

1. Draw the children's attention to the Word Search at the bottom of page 47. Set children the challenge of finding ten **ie** and **igh** words in the Word Search. Eight of the words run horizontally from left to right and two words run vertically from top to bottom.
2. Tell the children to circle each word as they find it and then write the words in two columns.

Answers:

t	a	m	l	i	e	k	d
i	h	e	o	h	i	g	h
e	p	n	i	g	h	t	j
b	l	i	g	h	t	q	p
c	r	i	e	d	g	s	i
t	r	i	e	d	c	u	e
n	f	b	r	i	g	h	t
r	i	g	h	t	r	t	i

ie	igh
tie	high
lie	night
pie	light
cried	bright
tried	right

Assessment: ie, igh

Tell the children that you are going to read out ten words, one at a time. Each word will be one of the **ie** or **igh** words that they have been learning. Tell the children that you will say the word, and then you will read out a sentence containing the word to help them know what it means. You will then repeat the word on its own before pausing so that the children can write the word down. For example: 1. **lie**. I told a little **lie**. **lie**

1. **lie**. I told a little **lie**. **lie**
2. **high**. Mum put the sweets up **high** on the shelf. **high**
3. **tie**. I learned how to **tie** my shoelaces. **tie**
4. **night**. At **night** I read my book. **night**
5. **pie**. I baked an apple **pie**. **pie**
6. **light**. I switched on the **light**. **light**
7. **cried**. I **cried** at the sad story. **cried**
8. **bright**. The sky is **bright** today. **bright**
9. **tried**. I **tried** to fall asleep. **tried**
10. **right**. Turn **right** at the corner to get to the park. **right**

For those students who need a bit more of a spelling challenge, read out the five further 'Quiet Zone' words to spell: **magpie, necktie, sigh, knight, flight**.

Full details of how to carry out assessment can be found on pages 6 and 108 of this guide.

STATION - WEEK 24
Royal Soil

OBJECTIVES
PART 1 – oy
Spell and use words in writing containing **oy**

Review previous learning
Ask the children if they can recall the spelling rule or any example words from the previous spelling lesson. Elicit ideas and remind the children that: The long vowel sound /igh/ can be spelt in many different ways. For example, **ie** as in **tie**, **igh** as in **night**, **i_e** as in **bike** and **y** as in **cry**.

Introducing the rule
Explain to the children that in today's lesson they will learn about words that are spelt with **oy**.

oy is used at the end of words and at the end of syllables.

> **Optional: Review the Letterland character stories**
> Character-based stories can help children to remember spelling patterns (see page 124).

Pupil Book Activity 1: Picture Match
1. Draw children's attention to the Word Bank at the top of page 48. Explain that all of these words contain **oy**.
2. Ask the children to read through the words in the Word Bank and talk to a partner about what they mean. Then ask the children if there are any words they are unsure of and explain the meanings to them, looking in the dictionary for a definition if necessary.
3. Ask the children to find and copy words from the Word Bank to match the pictures.

Answers: a) royal; b) boy; c) annoyed; d) toy; e) joy; f) Roy

Pupil Book Activity 2: Underline oy
1. Model the activity by choosing a word from the Word Bank and writing it on the board, for example: **boy**. Then underline the **oy** part of the word: b**oy**.
2. Ask the children to underline the **oy** spelling pattern in all of the words in the Word Bank.

Pupil Book Activity 3: Complete the Sentences
1. Read sentences **a – e** to the children, pausing as you reach each gap. Complete the first sentence with the children by re-reading to the first gap and then say: *Look at the Word Bank. Which word is something that a little sister might do?* Elicit children's ideas and establish that the word is **annoy**.
2. Ask the children to fill in the gaps in the rest of the sentences independently or with a partner.

Answers: a) annoy; b) boy; c) royal; d) joy; e) toy

Pupil Book Activity 4: Challenge!
1. Set the children the challenge of writing their own short story using **oy** words. Explain to the children that using the words in this way will help them to remember the words more effectively. Encourage the children to include as many of the Word Bank words as possible.
2. Use the following text as a model to show the children how to write the short story or, alternatively, use the text as a passage dictation by reading each sentence slowly and clearly for the children to

write down:

The **royal** family **enjoyed** watching the grand show every year. However this year, **Roy**, the head of the **royal** family, was **annoyed** because the tickets were sold out. He said he would give Dan the **boy** a new **toy** if he could find some spare tickets.

Review previous learning

Ask the children if they can recall the spelling rule or any example words from the previous spelling lesson. Elicit ideas and remind the children that: **oy** is used at the end of words and at the end of syllables.

OBJECTIVES
PART 2 – oi
Spell and use words in writing containing **oi**

Introducing the rule

Explain to the children that in today's lesson they will learn about words that are spelt with **oi**.

The digraph **oi** is virtually never used at the end of English words.

Optional: Review the Letterland character stories

Character-based stories can help children to remember spelling patterns (see page 124).

Pupil Book Activity 1: Picture Match

1. Draw the children's attention to the Word Bank at the top of page 49. Explain that all of these words contain **oi**.
2. Ask the children to read through the words in the Word Bank and talk to a partner about what they mean. Then ask the children if there are any words they are unsure of and explain the meanings to them, looking in the dictionary for a definition if necessary.
3. Ask the children to find and copy words from the Word Bank to match the pictures.

Answers: a) toilet; b) point; c) oil

Pupil Book Activity 2: Word Match

1. Draw the children's attention to the words written underneath the blank drawing boxes.
2. Ask the children to read each word and talk to a partner about what they mean.
3. Ask the children to draw a simple picture to match the words underneath each box, for example, to match the word 'join', children could draw themselves joining two items together.

Pupil Book Activity 3: Complete the Sentences

1. Read sentences **a – e** to the children, pausing as you reach each gap. Complete the first sentence with the children by re-reading to the first gap and then say: *Look at the Word Bank. Which word is something that might be put in a pan to help with cooking?* Elicit the children's ideas and establish that the word is **oil**.
2. Ask the children to fill in the gaps in the rest of the sentences independently or with a partner.

Answers: a) oil; b) join; c) coin; d) avoid; e) boil

Pupil Book Activity 4: Challenge!

1. Draw the children's attention to the Word Search at the bottom of page 49. Set children the

challenge of finding ten **oy** and **oi** words in the Word Search. Eight of the words run horizontally from left to right and two words run vertically from top to bottom.

2. Tell the children to circle each word as they find it and then write the words in two columns.

Answers:

b	a	k	p	o	i	l	o
o	j	e	n	j	o	y	c
y	q	a	n	n	o	y	i
d	j	o	i	n	f	n	w
e	r	t	b	c	o	i	n
j	o	y	g	u	z	m	t
s	p	o	i	n	t	v	o
l	h	s	o	i	l	x	y

oy	oi
boy	oil
enjoy	join
joy	coin
toy	point
annoy	soil

Assessment: oy, oi

Tell the children that you are going to read out ten words, one at a time. Each word will be one of the **oy** or **oi** words that they have been learning. Tell the children that you will say the word, and then you will read out a sentence containing the word to help them know what it means. You will then repeat the word on its own before pausing so that the children can write the word down. For example: 1. **boy**. Tom is the new **boy** in our class. **boy**

1. **boy**. Tom is the new **boy** in our class. **boy**
2. **toy**. Dad bought me a new **toy** car. **toy**
3. **oil**. Mum put **oil** in the car. **oil**
4. **join**. I would like to **join** a tennis club. **join**
5. **enjoy**. I **enjoy** swimming. **enjoy**
6. **annoy**. There is nothing that can **annoy** me. **annoy**
7. **coin**. I put the **coin** in my money bank. **coin**
8. **point**. I will **point** when I see the bird again. **point**
9. **joy**. I heard a squeal of **joy**. **joy**
10. **soil**. Fred dug in the **soil**. **soil**

For those students who need a bit more of a spelling challenge, read out the five further 'Quiet Zone' words to spell: **enjoyed, annoyed, toilet, joint, avoid**.

Full details of how to carry out assessment can be found on pages 6 and 108 of this guide.

STATION - WEEK 25

Short Shore

OBJECTIVES
PART 1 – or
Spell and use words in writing containing **or**

Review previous learning

Ask the children if they can recall the spelling rule or any example words from the previous spelling lesson. Elicit ideas and remind the children that: The digraph **oi** is virtually never used at the end of English words.

Introducing the rule

Explain to the children that in today's lesson they will learn about words that are spelt with **or**.

The sound /or/ can be spelt in many different ways. The most common spelling patterns for the /or/ sound are **or** as in **fork** and **ore** as in **more**.

Optional: Review the Letterland character stories

Character-based stories can help children to remember spelling patterns (see page 124).

Pupil Book Activity 1: Picture Match

1. Draw children's attention to the Word Bank at the top of page 50. Explain that all of these words contain **or**.
2. Ask the children to read through the words in the Word Bank and talk to a partner about what they mean. Then ask the children if there are any words they are unsure of and explain the meanings to them, looking in the dictionary for a definition if necessary.
3. Ask the children to find and copy words from the Word Bank to match the pictures.

Answers: a) horse; b) corn; c) storm; d) fork; e) thorn; f) story

Pupil Book Activity 2: Underline or

1. Model the activity by choosing a word from the Word Bank and writing it on the board, for example: **fork**. Then underline the **or** part of the word: **fork**.
2. Ask the children to underline the **or** spelling pattern in all of the words in the Word Bank.

Pupil Book Activity 3: Complete the Sentences

1. Read sentences **a – e** to the children, pausing as you reach each gap. Complete the first sentence with the children by re-reading to the first gap and then say: Look at the Word Bank. Which word is something that you could prick your finger on? Elicit children's ideas and establish that the word is **thorn**.
2. Ask the children to fill in the gaps in the rest of the sentences independently or with a partner.

Answers: a) thorn; b) horse; c) morning; d) fork; e) storm

Pupil Book Activity 4: Challenge!

1. Set the children the challenge of writing their own short story using **or** words. Explain to the children that using the words in this way will help them to remember the words more effectively. Encourage the children to include as many of the Word Bank words as possible.

2. Use the following text as a model to show the children how to write the short story or, alternatively, use the text as a passage dictation by reading each sentence slowly and clearly for the children to write down:

In the morning a **storm** blew over the **corn**. The **horse** hid in the barn. There was a rumble of thunder and a flash of **fork** lightning in the sky. Ted hid behind the **thorn** bush until he could run over to the barn and **sort** out the animals.

Watch Out!

Draw children's attention to the Watch Out! box at the bottom of page 50. Explain to the children that the /or/ sound can be spelt in 12 different ways. Some more examples are **oar** as in **soar**, **oor** as in **door** and **our** as in **pour**.

Review previous learning

Ask the children if they can recall the spelling rule or any example words from the previous spelling lesson. Elicit ideas and remind the children that: The sound /or/ can be spelt in many different ways. The most common spelling patterns for the /or/ sound are **or** as in **fork** and **ore** as in **more**.

Introducing the rule

Explain to the children that in today's lesson they will learn about words that are spelt with **ore**.

> **OBJECTIVES**
> **PART 2 – ore**
> Spell and use words in writing containing ore

> **Optional:** Review the Letterland character stories
> Character-based stories can help children to remember spelling patterns (see page 124).

Pupil Book Activity 1: Picture Match

1. Draw the children's attention to the Word Bank at the top of page 51. Explain that all of these words contain **ore**.
2. Ask the children to read through the words in the Word Bank and talk to a partner about what they mean. Then ask the children if there are any words they are unsure of and explain the meanings to them, looking in the dictionary for a definition if necessary.
3. Ask the children to find and copy words from the Word Bank to match the pictures.

Answers: a) snore; b) core; c) chore

Pupil Book Activity 2: Word Match

1. Draw the children's attention to the words written underneath the blank drawing boxes.
2. Ask the children to read each word and talk to a partner about what they mean.
3. Ask the children to draw a simple picture to match the words underneath each box, for example, to match the word 'wore', children could draw an outfit that they recently wore.

Pupil Book Activity 3: Complete the Sentences

1. Read sentences **a – e** to the children, pausing as you reach each gap. Complete the first sentence

with the children by re-reading to the first gap and then say: Look at the Word Bank. Which word is something that you might or might not do when you sleep? Elicit the children's ideas and establish that the word is **snore**.

2. Ask the children to fill in the gaps in the rest of the sentences independently or with a partner.

Answers: a) snore; b) more; c) before; d) score; e) tore

Pupil Book Activity 4: Challenge!

1. Draw the children's attention to the Word Search at the bottom of page 51. Set children the challenge of finding ten **or** and **ore** words in the Word Search. Eight of the words run horizontally from left to right and two words run vertically from top to bottom.
2. Tell the children to circle each word as they find it and then write the words in two columns.

Answers:

c	j	e	m	o	r	e	m
k	b	o	r	n	i	b	s
f	d	h	o	r	s	e	h
o	s	t	o	r	m	h	o
r	l	s	c	o	r	e	r
k	b	e	f	o	r	e	t
o	f	w	o	r	e	g	n
a	p	s	h	o	r	e	r

or	ore
fork	more
born	score
horse	before
storm	wore
short	shore

Assessment: or, ore

Tell the children that you are going to read out ten words, one at a time. Each word will be one of the **or** or **ore** words that they have been learning. Tell the children that you will say the word, and then you will read out a sentence containing the word to help them know what it means. You will then repeat the word on its own before pausing so that the children can write the word down. For example: 1. **fork**. I ate my dinner with a **fork**. **fork**

1. **fork**. I ate my dinner with a **fork**. **fork**
2. **more**. When the show finished we wanted to see **more**. **more**
3. **short**. I am not tall, I am **short**. **short**
4. **born**. A baby was **born** here yesterday. **born**
5. **score**. We got a top **score** in the match. **score**
6. **horse**. I watched the **horse** eating hay. **horse**
7. **tore**. My brother **tore** my homework. **tore**
8. **wore**. My gran **wore** her favourite skirt. **wore**
9. **morning**. I am going to the dentist in the **morning**. **morning**
10. **shore**. The waves lapped the **shore**. **shore**

For those students who need a bit more of a spelling challenge, read out the five further 'Quiet Zone' words to spell: **important**, **story**, **sword**, **before**, **chore**.

Full details of how to carry out assessment can be found on pages 6 and 108 of this guide.

Station - Week 26
Naughty Hawk

OBJECTIVES
PART 1 – au
Spell and use words in writing containing au

Review previous learning

Ask the children if they can recall the spelling rule or any example words from the previous spelling lesson. Elicit ideas and remind the children that: The sound /or/ can be spelt in many different ways. The most common spelling patterns for the /or/ sound are **or** as in **fork** and **ore** as in **more**.

Introducing the rule

Explain to the children that in today's lesson they will learn about words that are spelt with **au**.

Use the spelling pattern **au** at the beginning or in the middle of words for the /au/ sound.

Optional: Review the Letterland character stories

Character-based stories can help children to remember spelling patterns (see page 124).

Pupil Book Activity 1: Picture Match

1. Draw children's attention to the Word Bank at the top of page 52. Explain that all of these words contain **au**.
2. Ask the children to read through the words in the Word Bank and talk to a partner about what they mean. Then ask the children if there are any words they are unsure of and explain the meanings to them, looking in the dictionary for a definition if necessary.
3. Ask the children to find and copy words from the Word Bank to match the pictures.

Answers: a) dinosaur; b) sauce; c) autumn; d) launch; e) astronaut; f) author

Pupil Book Activity 2: Underline au

1. Model the activity by choosing a word from the Word Bank and writing it on the board, for example: **author**. Then underline the **au** part of the word: **author**.
2. Ask the children to underline the **au** spelling pattern in all of the words in the Word Bank.

Pupil Book Activity 3: Complete the Sentences

1. Read sentences **a** – **e** to the children, pausing as you reach each gap. Complete the first sentence with the children by re-reading to the first gap and then say: Look at the Word Bank. Which word is someone who writes stories? Elicit children's ideas and establish that the word is **author**.
2. Ask the children to fill in the gaps in the rest of the sentences independently or with a partner.

Answers: a) author; b) astronaut; c) August; d) pause; e) taut

Pupil Book Activity 4: Challenge!

1. Set the children the challenge of writing their own short story using **au** words. Explain to the children that using the words in this way will help them to remember the words more effectively. Encourage the children to include as many of the Word Bank words as possible.
2. Use the following text as a model to show the children how to write the short story or, alternatively, use the text as a passage dictation by reading each sentence slowly and clearly for the children to

write down:

The **author** had an idea for a new story. He decided he would write about an **astronaut** who, one **autumn**, **launched** into space and landed on a planet full of **dinosaurs**.

Watch Out!

Draw children's attention to the Think about it! box at the bottom of page 52. Explain to the children that depending on your accent you might hear the spelling pattern **au** as an /or/ sound instead of an /au/ sound.

Review previous learning

Ask the children if they can recall the spelling rule or any example words from the previous spelling lesson. Elicit ideas and remind the children that: The spelling pattern **au** is used at the beginning or in the middle of words for the /au/ sound.

**OBJECTIVES
PART 2 – aw
Spell and use words in writing containing aw**

Introducing the rule

Explain to the children that in today's lesson they will learn about words that are spelt with **aw**.

Use the spelling pattern **aw** at the end of words for the /au/ sound. If a single **l**, **n** or **k** follows the /au/ sound at the end of the word, use **aw**.

Optional: Review the Letterland character stories

Character-based stories can help children to remember spelling patterns (see page 124).

Pupil Book Activity 1: Picture Match

1. Draw the children's attention to the Word Bank at the top of page 53. Explain that all of these words contain **aw**.
2. Ask the children to read through the words in the Word Bank and talk to a partner about what they mean. Then ask the children if there are any words they are unsure of and explain the meanings to them, looking in the dictionary for a definition if necessary.
3. Ask the children to find and copy words from the Word Bank to match the pictures.

Answers: a) yawn; b) jaw; c) draw

Pupil Book Activity 2: Word Match

1. Draw the children's attention to the words written underneath the blank drawing boxes.
2. Ask the children to read each word and talk to a partner about what they mean.
3. Ask the children to draw a simple picture to match the words underneath each box, for example, to match the word 'straw', children could draw themselves drinking through a straw.

Pupil Book Activity 3: Complete the Sentences

1. Read sentences **a – e** to the children, pausing as you reach each gap. Complete the first sentence with the children by re-reading to the first gap and then say: Look at the Word Bank. Which word is something that a baby might do on its hands and knees? Elicit the children's ideas and establish that the word is **crawl**.

2. Ask the children to fill in the gaps in the rest of the sentences independently or with a partner.
Answers: a) crawl; b) awful; c) saw; d) shawl; e) straw

Pupil Book Activity 4: Challenge!

1. Draw the children's attention to the Word Search at the bottom of page 53. Set children the challenge of finding ten **au** and **aw** words in the Word Search. Eight of the words run horizontally from left to right and two words run vertically from top to bottom.
2. Tell the children to circle each word as they find it and then write the words in two columns.

Answers:

a	u	t	h	o	r	g	s
k	n	d	r	a	w	c	a
s	l	f	y	a	w	n	u
a	c	r	a	w	l	m	c
w	d	j	j	a	w	i	e
e	p	a	u	s	e	o	b
l	a	u	n	c	h	a	h
d	i	n	o	s	a	u	r

au	aw
author	draw
sauce	saw
pause	jaw
launch	crawl
dinosaur	jaw

Think about it!

Draw children's attention to the Think about it! box at the bottom of page 53. Explain to the children that depending on your accent you might hear the spelling pattern **au** as an /or/ sound instead of an /au/ sound.

Assessment: au, aw

Tell the children that you are going to read out ten words, one at a time. Each word will be one of the **au** or **aw** words that they have been learning. Tell the children that you will say the word, and then you will read out a sentence containing the word to help them know what it means. You will then repeat the word on its own before pausing so that the children can write the word down. For example:
1. **author**. The **author** wrote a new story. **author**

1. **author**. The **author** wrote a new story. **author**
2. **pause**. I **pause** when I see a full stop. **pause**
3. **haul**. The pirates had a treasure **haul**. **haul**
4. **saw**. I **saw** an eagle flying. **saw**
5. **draw**. I like to **draw** cats. **draw**
6. **yawn**. When I get tired I **yawn**. **yawn**
7. **autumn**. My favourite season is **autumn**. **autumn**
8. **sauce**. I like tomato **sauce** on my chips. **sauce**
9. **crawl**. The baby learned to **crawl**. **crawl**
10. **jaw**. My **jaw** aches from talking too much. **jaw**

For those students who need a bit more of a spelling challenge, read out the five further 'Quiet Zone' words to spell: **August, dinosaur, astronaut, shawl, squawk.**

STATION - WEEK 27
Airport Near

OBJECTIVES
PART 1 - air
Spell and use words in writing containing **air**

Review previous learning

Ask the children if they can recall the spelling rule or any example words from the previous spelling lesson. Elicit ideas and remind the children that the spelling pattern **aw** is used at the end of words for the /au/ sound. If a single **l**, **n** or **k** follows the /au/ sound at the end of the word, use **aw**.

Introducing the rule

Explain to the children that in today's lesson they will learn about words that are spelt with **air**.

The sound /air/ can be spelt in different ways. For example, **air** as in **hair**, **are** as in **care** and **ear** as in **bear**.

> **Optional: Review the Letterland character stories**
> Character-based stories can help children to remember spelling patterns (see page 124).

Pupil Book Activity 1: Picture Match

1. Draw children's attention to the Word Bank at the top of page 54. Explain that all of these words contain **air**.
2. Ask the children to read through the words in the Word Bank and talk to a partner about what they mean. Then ask the children if there are any words they are unsure of and explain the meanings to them, looking in the dictionary for a definition if necessary.
3. Ask the children to find and copy words from the Word Bank to match the pictures.

Answers: a) hair; b) pair; c) aircraft; d) chair; e) stairs; f) repair

Pupil Book Activity 2: Underline air

1. Model the activity by choosing a word from the Word Bank and writing it on the board, for example: **fair**. Then underline the **air** part of the word: f<u>air</u>.
2. Ask the children to underline the **air** spelling pattern in all of the words in the Word Bank.

Pupil Book Activity 3: Complete the Sentences

1. Read sentences **a – e** to the children, pausing as you reach each gap. Complete the first sentence with the children by re-reading to the first gap and then say: Look at the Word Bank. Which word is somewhere that a bear might be? Elicit children's ideas and establish that the word is **lair**.
2. Ask the children to fill in the gaps in the rest of the sentences independently or with a partner.

Answers: a) lair; b) hair; c) dairy; d) air; e) chair

Pupil Book Activity 4: Challenge!

1. Set the children the challenge of writing their own short story using **air** words. Explain to the children that using the words in this way will help them to remember the words more effectively. Encourage the children to include as many of the Word Bank words as possible.
2. Use the following text as a model to show the children how to write the short story or, alternatively,

use the text as a passage dictation by reading each sentence slowly and clearly for the children to write down:

The girl with **fair hair** sat on the **chair**. She ate her **dairy eclair** and looked out of the window. She watched an **aircraft** fly overhead. Then she went up the **stairs** to **repair** the bed she had broken earlier.

Review previous learning

Ask the children if they can recall the spelling rule or any example words from the previous spelling lesson. Elicit ideas and remind the children that: The sound /air/ can be spelt in different ways. For example, **air** as in **hair**, **are** as in **care** and **ear** as in **bear**.

**OBJECTIVES
PART 2 – ear
Spell and use words in writing containing ear**

Introducing the rule

Explain to the children that in today's lesson they will learn about words that are spelt with **ear** when it represents an /ear/ sound.

The letters **ear** can represent the sound /ear/ as in **dear** but they can also represent the sounds /air/ as in **bear** and /er/ as in **earth**.

Optional: Review the Letterland character stories

Character-based stories can help children to remember spelling patterns (see page 124).

Pupil Book Activity 1: Picture Match

1. Draw the children's attention to the Word Bank at the top of page 55. Explain that all of these words contain **ear**.
2. Ask the children to read through the words in the Word Bank and talk to a partner about what they mean. Then ask the children if there are any words they are unsure of and explain the meanings to them, looking in the dictionary for a definition if necessary.
3. Ask the children to find and copy words from the Word Bank to match the pictures.

Answers: a) beard; b) hear; c) tear

Pupil Book Activity 2: Word Match

1. Draw the children's attention to the words written underneath the blank drawing boxes.
2. Ask the children to read each word and talk to a partner about what they mean.
3. Ask the children to draw a simple picture to match the words underneath each box, for example, to match the word 'hear', children could draw something that they can hear.

Pupil Book Activity 3: Complete the Sentences

1. Read sentences **a** – **e** to the children, pausing as you reach each gap. Complete the first sentence with the children by re-reading to the first gap and then say: Look at the Word Bank. Which word is something that a farmer might use to cut a sheep's wool? Elicit the children's ideas and establish that the word is **shears**.
2. Ask the children to fill in the gaps in the rest of the sentences independently or with a partner.

Answers: a) shears; b) hear; c) near; d) year; e) beard

Pupil Book Activity 4: Challenge!

Draw the children's attention to the Word Search at the bottom of page 55. Set children the challenge of finding ten **air** and **ear** words in the Word Search. Eight of the words run horizontally from left to right and two words run vertically from top to bottom.

Tell the children to circle each word as they find it and then write the words in two columns.

Answers:

a	l	p	a	i	r	s	f
i	b	q	d	e	a	r	a
r	g	h	a	i	r	f	i
p	h	e	a	r	c	j	r
m	i	o	b	e	a	r	d
c	h	a	i	r	d	t	k
x	v	n	e	a	r	e	u
a	h	w	n	y	e	a	r

air	ear
air	dear
pair	hear
hair	beard
fair	near
chair	year

Think about it!

Draw children's attention to the Think about it! box on page 55. Ask the children if they can explain the different meanings of **dear** and **deer**, and **hear** and **here**. Write the words on the board so they can see and refer to the spellings.

Assessment: air, ear

Tell the children that you are going to read out ten words, one at a time. Each word will be one of the **air** or **ear** words that they have been learning. Tell the children that you will say the word, and then you will read out a sentence containing the word to help them know what it means. You will then repeat the word on its own before pausing so that the children can write the word down. For example:
1. **air**. I took a deep breath of **air**. **air**

1. **air**. I took a deep breath of **air**. **air**
2. **dear**. Grandmother always call me '**dear**'. **dear**
3. **hear**. I **hear** people on the stairs. **hear**
4. **fair**. Alison has **fair** hair. **fair**
5. **beard**. Dad got his **beard** trimmed. **beard**
6. **near**. We walked **near** the lake. **near**
7. **pair**. I can't find a **pair** of matching socks. **pair**
8. **hair**. My gran has curly **hair**. **hair**
9. **chair**. I like to sit in the rocking **chair**. **chair**
10. **year**. I have studied hard all **year**. **year**

For those students who need a bit more of a spelling challenge, read out the five further 'Quiet Zone' words to spell: **dairy, repair, upstairs, shears, earrings**.

Full details of how to carry out assessment can be found on pages 6 and 108 of this guide.

STATION - WEEK 28
Sh**are** P**ear**s

OBJECTIVES
PART 1 – are
Spell and use words in writing containing **are**

Review previous learning
Ask the children if they can recall the spelling rule or any example words from the previous spelling lesson. Elicit ideas and remind the children that: The letters **ear** can represent the sound /ear/ as in **dear** but they can also represent the sounds /air/ as in **bear** and /er/ as in **earth**.

Introducing the rule
Explain to the children that in today's lesson they will learn about words that are spelt with **are** when it represents an /air/ sound.

The sound /air/ can be spelt in different ways. For example, **air** as in **hair**, **are** as in **care** and **ear** as in **bear**.

Optional: Review the Letterland character stories
Character-based stories can help children to remember spelling patterns (see page 124).

Pupil Book Activity 1: Picture Match
1. Draw children's attention to the Word Bank at the top of page 56. Explain that all of these words contain **are**.
2. Ask the children to read through the words in the Word Bank and talk to a partner about what they mean. Then ask the children if there are any words they are unsure of and explain the meanings to them, looking in the dictionary for a definition if necessary.
3. Ask the children to find and copy words from the Word Bank to match the pictures.

Answers: a) hare; b) square; c) mare; d) care; e) share; f) stare

Pupil Book Activity 2: Underline are
1. Model the activity by choosing a word from the Word Bank and writing it on the board, for example: **bare**. Then underline the <u>**are**</u> part of the word: b<u>**are**</u>.
2. Ask the children to underline the **are** spelling pattern in all of the words in the Word Bank.

Pupil Book Activity 3: Complete the Sentences
1. Read sentences **a – e** to the children, pausing as you reach each gap. Complete the first sentence with the children by re-reading to the first gap and then say: Look at the Word Bank. Which word means female horse? Elicit children's ideas and establish that the word is **mare**.
2. Ask the children to fill in the gaps in the rest of the sentences independently or with a partner.

Answers: a) mare; b) scared; c) care; d) spare; e) square

Pupil Book Activity 4: Challenge!
1. Set the children the challenge of writing their own short story using **are** words. Explain to the children that using the words in this way will help them to remember the words more effectively. Encourage the children to include as many of the Word Bank words as possible.

2. Use the following text as a model to show the children how to write the short story or, alternatively, use the text as a passage dictation by reading each sentence slowly and clearly for the children to write down:

The **mare** asked the **hare**, 'Why do you **stare** at me?' The **hare** explained that it was **scared** of the **mare**. The **mare** told the **hare** not to feel **scared**. She would **share** her **square** field to show that she **cared**.

Think about it!

Draw children's attention to the Think about it! box at the bottom of page 56. Ask the children if they can explain the different meanings of **bare** and **bear**, and **hare** and **hair**. Write the words on the board so they can see and refer to the spellings.

> **OBJECTIVES**
> **PART 2 – ear**
> **Spell and use words in writing containing ear**

Review previous learning

Ask the children if they can recall the spelling rule or any example words from the previous spelling lesson. Elicit ideas and remind the children that: The sound /air/ can be spelt in different ways. For example, **air** as in **hair**, **are** as in **care** and **ear** as in **bear**.

Introducing the rule

Explain to the children that in today's lesson they will learn about words that are spelt with **ear** when it represents an /air/ sound. Explain that this spelling is uncommon and there are not many examples. Show the Word Bank and explain that there also a few words that are spelt **ear** but have the sound /er/.

Optional: Review the Letterland character stories
Character-based stories can help children to remember spelling patterns (see page 124).

Pupil Book Activity 1: Picture Match

1. Draw the children's attention to the Word Bank at the top of page 57. Explain that all of these words contain **ear**.
2. Ask the children to read through the words in the Word Bank and talk to a partner about what they mean. Then ask the children if there are any words they are unsure of and explain the meanings to them, looking in the dictionary for a definition if necessary.
3. Ask the children to find and copy words from the Word Bank to match the pictures.

Answers: a) bear; b) pear; c) tear

Pupil Book Activity 2: Word Match

1. Draw the children's attention to the words written underneath the blank drawing boxes. Tell the children that in these words the **ear** spelling represents an /er/ sound.
2. Ask the children to read each word and talk to a partner about what they mean.
3. Ask the children to draw a simple picture to match the words underneath each box, for example, to match the word 'early', children could draw themselves getting up in the morning.

Pupil Book Activity 3: Complete the Sentences

1. Read sentences **a – e** to the children, pausing as you reach each gap. Complete the first sentence with the children by re-reading to the first gap and then say: Look at the Word Bank. Which word means the same as 'promise'? Elicit the children's ideas and establish that the word is **swear**.
2. Ask the children to fill in the gaps in the rest of the sentences independently or with a partner.

Answers: a) swear; b) pear; c) wear; d) tear; e) bear

Pupil Book Activity 4: Challenge!

1. Draw the children's attention to the Word Search at the bottom of page 57. Set children the challenge of finding ten **are** and **ear** words in the Word Search. Eight of the words run horizontally from left to right and two words run vertically from top to bottom.
2. Tell the children to circle each word as they find it and then write the words in two columns.

Answers:

c	a	r	e	o	a	n	d
e	k	b	e	a	r	u	a
s	c	a	r	e	d	i	r
t	f	p	e	a	r	b	e
b	l	d	h	w	e	a	r
a	p	t	e	a	r	c	j
r	s	w	e	a	r	m	r
e	g	q	s	h	a	r	e

are	ear
care	bear
scared	pear
dare	wear
bare	swear
share	tear

Think about it!

Draw children's attention to the Think about it! box on page 57. Ask the children if they can explain the different meanings of **pear** and **pair**, and **tear** and **tear**. Write the words on the board so they can see and refer to the spellings.

Assessment: are, ear

Tell the children that you are going to read out ten words, one at a time. Each word will be one of the **are** or **ear** words that they have been learning. Tell the children that you will say the word, and then you will read out a sentence containing the word to help them know what it means. You will then repeat the word on its own before pausing so that the children can write the word down. For example:
1. **bare**. The tree was **bare** after the leaves fell off. **bare**

1. **bare**. The tree was **bare** after the leaves fell off. **bare**
2. **dare**. I **dare** you to sing a song. **dare**
3. **bear**. The **bear** ate the honey. **bear**
4. **pear**. I have a little **pear** tree. **pear**
5. **wear**. I like to **wear** shorts. **wear**
6. **care**. I **care** about animals. **care**
7. **tear**. My book has a **tear** on one of the pages. **tear**
8. **swear**. I **swear** to be a kind person. **swear**
9. **share**. My sister won't **share** her sweets. **share**
10. **spare**. Our car has a **spare** tire. **spare**

For those students who need a bit more of a spelling challenge, read out the five further 'Quiet Zone' words to spell: **scared**, **aware**, **square**, **early**, **earth**.

STATION - WEEK 29
Dolphin Whistle

OBJECTIVES
PART 1 – ph
Spell and use words in writing containing **ph**

Review previous learning

Ask the children if they can recall the spelling rule or any example words from the previous spelling lesson. Elicit ideas and remind the children that: The sound /air/ can be spelt in different ways. For example, **air** as in **hair**, **are** as in **care** and **ear** as in **bear**.

Introducing the rule

Explain to the children that in today's lesson they will learn about words that are spelt with **ph**.

The sound /f/ is not usually spelt as **ph** in short everyday words such as **fat**, **fill**, **fun**.

> **Optional: Review the Letterland character stories**
> Character-based stories can help children to remember spelling patterns (see page 124).

Pupil Book Activity 1: Picture Match

1. Draw children's attention to the Word Bank at the top of page 58. Explain that all of these words contain **ph**.
2. Ask the children to read through the words in the Word Bank and talk to a partner about what they mean. Then ask the children if there are any words they are unsure of and explain the meanings to them, looking in the dictionary for a definition if necessary.
3. Ask the children to find and copy words from the Word Bank to match the pictures.

Answers: a) trophy; b) elephant; c) dolphin; d) phone; e) photo; f) alphabet

Pupil Book Activity 2: Underline ph

1. Model the activity by choosing a word from the Word Bank and writing it on the board, for example: **dolphin**. Then underline the **ph** part of the word: **dolphin**.
2. Ask the children to underline the **ph** spelling pattern in all of the words in the Word Bank.

Pupil Book Activity 3: Complete the Sentences

1. Read sentences **a – e** to the children, pausing as you reach each gap. Complete the first sentence with the children by re-reading to the first gap and then say: *Look at the Word Bank. Which word is something that you can hear ringing?* Elicit children's ideas and establish that the word is **phone**.
2. Ask the children to fill in the gaps in the rest of the sentences independently or with a partner.

Answers: a) phone; b) elephant; c) alphabet; d) trophy; e) photo

Pupil Book Activity 4: Challenge!

1. Set the children the challenge of writing their own short story using **ph** words. Explain to the children that using the words in this way will help them to remember the words more effectively. Encourage the children to include as many of the Word Bank words as possible.
2. Use the following text as a model to show the children how to write the short story or, alternatively, use the text as a passage dictation by reading each sentence slowly and clearly for the children to

101

write down:

Samira took a **photo** of the **elephant**. Then she walked over to see the **dolphins** in the big pool. The **dolphins** were amazing. They won a **trophy** because they knew the letters of the **alphabet**. The **dolphins** were both **orphans**. Later Samira **phoned** her gran to tell her about her visit to the wildlife park.

Review previous learning

Ask the children if they can recall the spelling rule or any example words from the previous spelling lesson. Elicit ideas and remind the children that: The sound /f/ is not usually spelt as **ph** in short everyday words such as **fat**, **fill**, **fun**.

> **OBJECTIVES**
> **PART 2 – wh**
> Spell and use words in writing containing **wh**

Introducing the rule

Explain to the children that in today's lesson they will learn about words that are spelt with **wh**.

The letters **wh** are usually used at the beginning of words for the /w/ sound. The letter **w** can be used for the /w/ sound at the beginning, middle or end.

Optional: Review the Letterland character stories

Character-based stories can help children to remember spelling patterns (see page 124).

Pupil Book Activity 1: Picture Match

1. Draw the children's attention to the Word Bank at the top of page 59. Explain that all of these words contain **wh**.
2. Ask the children to read through the words in the Word Bank and talk to a partner about what they mean. Then ask the children if there are any words they are unsure of and explain the meanings to them, looking in the dictionary for a definition if necessary.
3. Ask the children to find and copy words from the Word Bank to match the pictures.

Answers: a) wheel; b) whale; c) whistle

Pupil Book Activity 2: Word Match

1. Draw the children's attention to the words written underneath the blank drawing boxes.
2. Ask the children to read each word and talk to a partner about what they mean.
3. Ask the children to draw a simple picture to match the words underneath each box, for example, to match the word 'white', children could draw something that is the colour white, for example, a polar bear or snowman.

Pupil Book Activity 3: Complete the Sentences

1. Read sentences **a – e** to the children, pausing as you reach each gap. Complete the first sentence with the children by re-reading to the first gap and then say: Look at the Word Bank. Which word is something that you might need to do if someone is sleeping? Elicit the children's ideas and establish that the word is **whisper**.
2. Ask the children to fill in the gaps in the rest of the sentences independently or with a partner.

Answers: a) whisper; b) when; c) whale; d) white; e) whistle

Pupil Book Activity 4: Challenge!

1. Draw the children's attention to the Word Search at the bottom of page 59. Set children the challenge of finding ten **ph** and **wh** words in the Word Search. Eight of the words run horizontally from left to right and two words run vertically from top to bottom.
2. Tell the children to circle each word as they find it and then write the words in two columns.

Answers:

a	d	p	h	o	n	e	w
l	h	p	h	o	t	o	h
p	w	h	e	r	e	c	e
h	p	h	o	b	i	a	n
a	e	w	h	i	c	h	g
b	w	h	e	e	l	f	b
e	i	a	w	h	i	t	e
t	t	y	p	h	o	o	n

ph	wh
phone	when
alphabet	where
phobia	which
typhoon	wheel
photo	white

Assessment: ph, wh

Tell the children that you are going to read out ten words, one at a time. Each word will be one of the **ph** or **wh** words that they have been learning. Tell the children that you will say the word, and then you will read out a sentence containing the word to help them know what it means. You will then repeat the word on its own before pausing so that the children can write the word down. For example:
1. **dolphin**. I saw the **dolphin** leaping in the sea. **dolphin**

1. **dolphin**. I saw the **dolphin** leaping in the sea. **dolphin**
2. **when**. I was happy **when** it was story time. **when**
3. **alphabet**. The **alphabet** has vowel and consonant letters. **alphabet**
4. **where**. I looked for my shoes **where** I thought I left them. **where**
5. **elephant**. The **elephant** squirted water everywhere. **elephant**
6. **which**. **Which** juice do you prefer? **Which**
7. **trophy**. My team won the **trophy**. **trophy**
8. **wheel**. My grandpa put a new **wheel** on the go-cart. **wheel**
9. **phone**. I heard my sister chatting on the **phone**. **phone**
10. **while**. The cat slept **while** the dog barked. **while**

For those students who need a bit more of a spelling challenge, read out the five further 'Quiet Zone' words to spell: **orphan**, **typhoon**, **white**, **whisper**, **whistle**.

Full details of how to carry out assessment can be found on pages 6 and 108 of this guide.

STATION - WEEK 30
Unusual Sunset

OBJECTIVES
PART 1 – un–

Spell and use words in writing containing the prefix un–

Review previous learning

Ask the children if they can recall the spelling rule or any example words from the previous spelling lesson. Elicit ideas and remind the children that: The letters **wh** are usually used at the beginning of words for the /w/ sound. The letter **w** can be used for the /w/ sound at the beginning, middle or end.

Introducing the rule

Explain to the children that in today's lesson they will learn about words that are spelt with **un**-.

The prefix **un**- is added to the beginning of a word without any change to the spelling of the root word.

> **Optional: Review the Letterland character stories**
>
> Character-based stories can help children to remember spelling patterns.

> **Optional: Review the Letterland Grammar analogies**
>
> Use the analogy to explain prefixes (see page 127).

Pupil Book Activity 1: Picture Match

1. Draw children's attention to the Word Bank at the top of page 60. Explain that all of these words contain **un**-.
2. Ask the children to read through the words in the Word Bank and talk to a partner about what they mean. Then ask the children if there are any words they are unsure of and explain the meanings to them, looking in the dictionary for a definition if necessary.
3. Ask the children to find and copy words from the Word Bank to match the pictures.

Answers: a) unwell; b) unload; c) unhappy; d) unfit; e) unlock; f) undo

Pupil Book Activity 2: Underline un-

1. Model the activity by choosing a word from the Word Bank and writing it on the board, for example: **unhappy**. Then underline the **un**- part of the word: **unhappy**
2. Ask the children to underline the **un**- spelling pattern in all of the words in the Word Bank.

Pupil Book Activity 3: Complete the Sentences

1. Read sentences **a** – **e** to the children, pausing as you reach each gap. Complete the first sentence with the children by re-reading to the first gap and then say: Look at the Word Bank. Which word is something that you can do to a door using a key? Elicit children's ideas and establish that the word is **unlock**.
2. Ask the children to fill in the gaps in the rest of the sentences independently or with a partner.

Answers: a) unlock; b) unfit; c) unhappy; d) unload; e) unwell

Pupil Book Activity 4: Challenge!

1. Set the children the challenge of writing their own short story using **un-** words. Explain to the children that using the words in this way will help them to remember the words more effectively. Encourage the children to include as many of the Word Bank words as possible.
2. Use the following text as a model to show the children how to write the short story or, alternatively, use the text as a passage dictation by reading each sentence slowly and clearly for the children to write down:

Deb was **unhappy**. She was dressing and **undressing** her dolls when mum asked her to do some jobs. She had to **undo** the the tangle of skipping ropes. Then she had to **unload** the bags from the car. Deb felt it was **unfair**. She said she felt **unwell** so her mum sent her to bed.

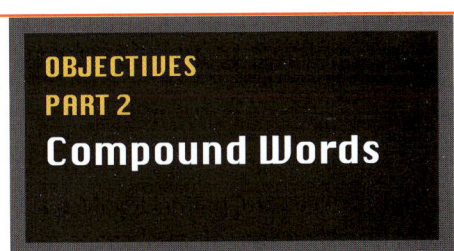

OBJECTIVES PART 2
Compound Words

Review previous learning

Ask the children if they can recall the spelling rule or any example words from the previous spelling lesson. Elicit ideas and remind the children that: The prefix **un-** is added to the beginning of a word without any change to the spelling of the root word.

Introducing the rule

Explain to the children that in today's lesson they will learn about words that are called **compound words**. Compound words are two words joined together. Each part of the longer word is spelt as it would be if it were on its own

> **Optional: Review the Letterland Grammar analogies**
> Use the analogy to explain compound nouns (see page 127).

Pupil Book Activity 1: Picture Match

1. Draw the children's attention to the Word Bank at the top of page 61. Explain that all of these words are **compound words**.
2. Ask the children to read through the words in the Word Bank and talk to a partner about what they mean. Then ask the children if there are any words they are unsure of and explain the meanings to them, looking in the dictionary for a definition if necessary.
3. Ask the children to find and copy words from the Word Bank to match the pictures.

Answers: a) blackberry; b) toothbrush; c) footprints

Pupil Book Activity 2: Word Match

1. Draw the children's attention to the words written underneath the blank drawing boxes.
2. Ask the children to read each word and talk to a partner about what they mean.
3. Ask the children to draw a simple picture to match the words underneath each box, for example, to match the word 'butterfly', children could draw a butterfly.

Pupil Book Activity 3: Complete the Sentences

1. Read sentences **a – e** to the children, pausing as you reach each gap. Complete the first sentence with the children by re-reading to the first gap and then say: Look at the Word Bank. Which word is something that you use to clean your teeth? Elicit the children's ideas and establish that the word is **toothbrush**.

2. Ask the children to fill in the gaps in the rest of the sentences independently or with a partner.
Answers: a) toothbrush; b) farmyard; c) sunset; d) football; e) blackberry

Pupil Book Activity 4: Challenge!

1. Draw the children's attention to the Word Search at the bottom of page 61. Set children the challenge of finding ten **un-** and **compound words** in the Word Search. Eight of the words run horizontally from left to right and two words run vertically from top to bottom.
2. Tell the children to circle each word as they find it and then write the words in two columns.

Answers:

u	u	n	l	o	c	k	u
n	u	n	w	e	l	l	n
f	u	n	l	o	a	d	d
i	s	u	n	s	e	t	o
t	r	a	i	n	b	o	w
f	o	o	t	b	a	l	l
f	a	r	m	y	a	r	d
b	e	d	r	o	o	m	a

Prefix -un	Compound Words
unfit	sunset
unlock	rainbow
undo	football
unwell	farmyard
unload	bedroom

Assessment: un-, compound words

Tell the children that you are going to read out ten words, one at a time. Each word will be one of the **un-** or **compound words** that they have been learning. Tell the children that you will say the word, and then you will read out a sentence containing the word to help them know what it means. You will then repeat the word on its own before pausing so that the children can write the word down. For example: 1. **unhappy**. I was **unhappy** when it rained all day. **unhappy**

1. **unhappy**. I was **unhappy** when it rained all day. **unhappy**
2. **undo**. I learned how to **undo** the knots. **undo**
3. **football**. We love playing **football**. **football**
4. **farmyard**. There are lots of animals at the **farmyard**. **farmyard**
5. **unload**. Mum asked me to **unload** the car. **unload**
6. **sunset**. We watched the lovely **sunset**. **sunset**
7. **unfair**. It was **unfair** that my sister got a new toy. **unfair**
8. **rainbow**. We saw a big **rainbow**. **rainbow**
9. **toothbrush**. My **toothbrush** is blue. **toothbrush**
10. **unlock**. I can **unlock** the door. **unlock**

For those students who need a bit more of a spelling challenge, read out the five further 'Quiet Zone' words to spell: **unafraid, unblock, playground, blackberry, butterfly**.

Full details of how to carry out assessment can be found on pages 6 and 108 of this guide.

Appendices

Assessment and Pupil Record Sheets 108-110

Spelling Certificate 111

Games & Activities 112-117

    Memory Trigger 112

    Choo choo! 113

    Trainspotter! 114

    Fill the seats! 116

Letterland Phonics 118-124

    What is Letterland Phonics? 118

    Scope of *Letterland Phonics Teacher's Guide* 119

    Abbreviated Letterland Phonics stories 120-124

Letterland Grammar 125-127

    What is Letterland Grammar? 125

    Scope of *Letterland Grammar Teacher's Guide* 126

Abbreviated Letterland Grammar stories 127

Assessment

As part of your weekly routine (generally a Friday activity), spellings should be assessed. To stop this being 'the dreaded test', introduce the idea of **Spelling Stations!**

Each child should have a copy of *Spelling Stations Ticket Book*. Each week they will be tested on the words from **one ticket**. Children will have covered the spelling patterns in class in their *Pupil Book*. Children should be encouraged to revise the spellings in the *Ticket Book* at home with a parent/carer.

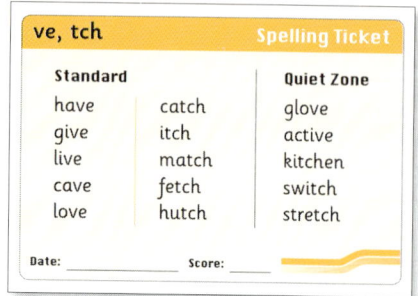

Proceedure

Teacher: At the start of the spelling test, you could say: **"Spelling Stations - Tickets Please!"** Collect in the *Ticket Books*. You could blow a whistle to signify the start and end of the test.

Teacher: Read out the 'Standard' Word Bank and sentences from the Assessment section of the *Teacher's Guide* to the children slowly. Repeat.

Students: Write their test answers in their own exercise book, or on a separate sheet of paper.

Teacher: Read out the five further 'Quiet Zone' words to spell for those in the class that need more of a spelling challenge. Remind the other children that they are in the 'Quiet Zone' and must stay quiet to help the other children concentrate.

Teacher: Collect all the student's answers to be marked.

Teacher: Mark the papers and keep a record of the spelling scores on the sheets provided on the next page or your own class record.

Teacher: Fill in the date (or use a date stamp) in each child's *Ticket Book* and their score. Return marked Spelling Tests to your students. Ask them to look at any errors they have made and write those words again in the space provided **on the back of their spelling ticket** so they (and their parents) have a record of how they are getting on with their spellings.

Differentiation

You will expect most students to learn the Standard list of 10 words per week, and the high achieving students to learn 15 words (both Standard and Quiet Zone). However you may discretely advise some students which portion of the list he or she is responsible for learning. For example, you could limit a student to only being expected to spell 5 Standard Words. They fully participate in class activities but are evaluated primarily on assigned words.

For students who are well below age-related expectations in reading and spelling, intervention at their instructional level is important.

Marking and scoring

- The Record Sheets are for STANDARD scores. Enter the total number of words spelled correctly out of 10.
- The target score for spelling is 80%.
- If a child is consistently scoring below 80%, colour the score boxes in red. Check if the student is fully understanding what is expected of them and if they are doing any work at home to consolidate their learning. Encourage them to play the spelling games on pages 112-117. If scores continue to fall below the target, consider reducing the number of spellings per week and look to other intervention strategies, such as revisiting the phonic structures using the *Letterland Phonics Teacher's Guide* to ensure those foundations are fully formed before progressing further.

Pupil Record Sheet 1

Letterland Spelling Stations Teacher's Guide - Year 1

Name	Week														
	1	2	3	4	5	6	7	8	9	10	11	12	13	14	15
Andrew C	8/10	7/10	6/10	9/10	9/10										

© Letterland International 2018. May be photocopied only for use within purchasing school.

Pupil Record Sheet 2

Letterland Spelling Stations Teacher's Guide - Year 1

Name	Week														
	16	17	18	19	20	21	22	23	24	25	26	27	28	29	30

© Letterland International 2018. May be photocopied only for use within purchasing school.

Spelling Stations Award – Platform 1

This award is being presented to

_____

for completing all of the spellings set this year.

Keep up the good work!

Signed _____ Date _____

Spelling Stations Award – Platform 1

This award is being presented to

_____

for completing all of the spellings set this year.

Keep up the good work!

Signed _____ Date _____

© Letterland International 2018. May be photocopied for use only within purchasing school.

Memory Trigger

The train station theme with memorable station names provides an association for the Word Banks. Each week has a station name and image associated with it. By remembering the station name, children have a visual clue to help them unlock the words of the week rather than simply remembering an abstract list of words.

Write a station name on the board, then invite children to come and add more words under each part of the station name using the same spelling patterns. See how long your lists can grow!

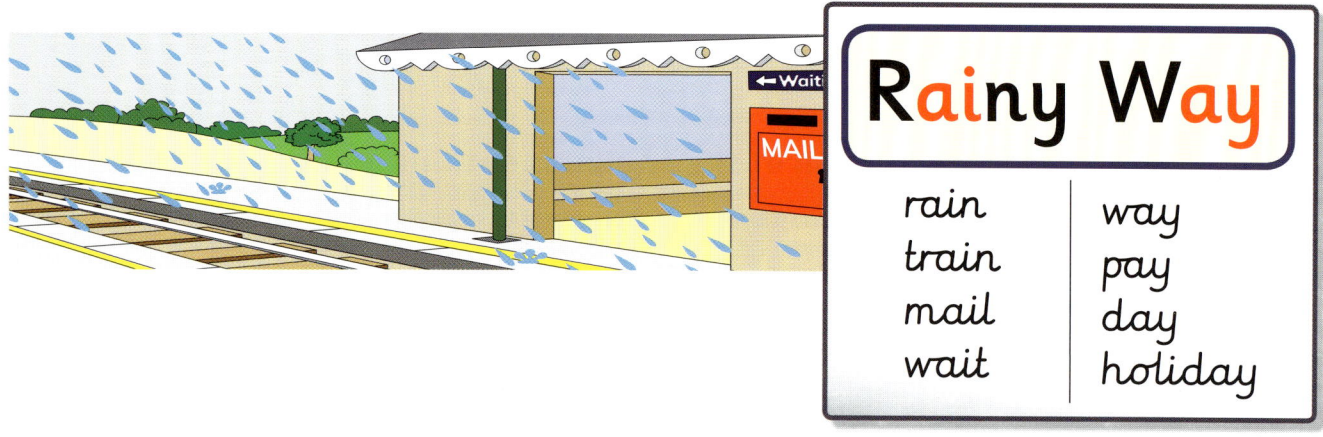

Rainy Way

rain	way
train	pay
mail	day
wait	holiday

Loud Town

shout	now
mouse	crowd
house	frown
scout	gown

Bike Zone

kite	cone
white	rose
lime	nose
pine	hose

Choo choo!

Number of players: Choo choo! is played with the teacher and two or three competing groups in the classroom.

Teacher needs: The weeks Word Bank, whiteboard or screen to write the words as children orally spell and to keep score. (A student could be the scorekeeper.)

Children need: If using option 2 or 4 below, children need their Word Bank.

Preparation: Choose a team to go first, perhaps by guessing a number from 1-10. Each group is arranged in a line, a circle or semi-circle—seated or standing. Each group needs a name or number to keep a tally of scores.

How to play

Teacher: Say a word from the Word Bank and ask the whole class to repeat it.

Group 1: The first child in the first group says the first letter in the word, the next child in the same group the second letter and so on until the last letter. The child that comes after the last letter says "**Choo choo!**"

Teacher: As children say each letter, write it on the board. If the group spells the word correctly and the last child says, "**Choo choo!**," the team gets one point. The next group receives the next word from the Word Bank.

One 'pass' allowed: If a child in the group is uncertain of the next letter, he or she can pass by simply saying "**Vowel**" or "**Consonant**." If the child has identified the type of letter correctly, then the next child can say the actual letter and so on. For each word, only one pass is allowed.

Errors: If a child misses a letter, the teacher immediately says **not quite right** and does not write the incorrect letter on the board. The next group then gets a chance to complete the word beginning with the letter after the last correct letter and with each child in turn saying one letter, etc. If they complete the word correctly and say "**Choo choo!**," their team gets a point.

Where to start the next round: After each word is completed, move to the next group. After each group has had their turn, go back to the first group and begin with the next child in the group to say an incorrect letter or to say, "**Choo choo**!"

Winning

The team with the most points wins. Tie scores are also celebrated.

Option

Give children a few minutes before they play to prepare using their Word Bank. Suggest they choose words that might be difficult, and try spelling aloud or writing them with a partner.

Train Spotter

Number of players: Two

Children need: Blank Train Spotter gameboard (page 113) and Word Bank.

Preparation: This is a train-themed version of battleships! On the upper grid, students write ten spelling words from the lists assigned by the teacher. You can write words across (left to right) and straight down. Across words and down words can only intersect where they share the same letter. Fold the page across the middle. Don't let your opponent see it. Face your opponent. You could use a book to block the view.

How to play

- **Spotting Trains:** The object of the game is to find your opponent's trains (words) in one of two ways.
- Call out a letter and a number from the grid ("Platform **G 2**" for example).
- Your opponent finds that space on their word grid. If there is a letter in that space, your opponent names the letter and you write that letter in the lower grid. Your opponent makes a light slash over the letter on their grid.
- If the space you called out is blank, your opponent says, "**miss**". You make a slash mark in that space on the lower grid on your game board.
- Then it's your opponent's turn to say a number and letter from the grid.
- When you have 'found' all the letters in the word, your opponent says, "**found**."
- After you have hit one or more letters in a word and you think you know the whole word, you can go for '**Train Spotter!**' on your next turn. First say what you think the word is. If you say the correct word, you have to spell the word correctly with you own paper hidden from your sight. If you are correct, your opponent says, "**Train Spotter!**" and must mark all the letters in the word as found and tell you which space the first letter belongs in so you can write the word on your grid.
- If you guess the wrong word or spell it incorrectly, your opponent tells you that you missed it you miss a turn.

Winning

- The first player to spot all the other player's trains is the winner.
- If time runs out before one of you find all the other's trains, you both count all the letters that have not been found on your own lower grid. The one with the most letters left is the winner.

Train Spotter!

Mark your misses / hits in the top grid. When you spot an opponent's train, they must tell you the letter to write in the space.

Write 10 spelling words on the grid below. Mark the letters that your opponent hits.

Fill the seats!

Number of players: Two (or three if number of students is odd).

Children need: Word Bank for the week, Fill the seats! gameboard (page 115, laminated or placed in a plastic protector) or each child can make their own paper set up for the game, dice for each pair.

How to play

Players roll the die. The person with the highest number goes first.

Player 1: Roll again.

Player 2: Call out any word from the Word Bank for Player 1 to spell.

Player 1: Writes the word on the seat that matches the number on the die.

Player 2: Checks opponent's spelling with the Word Bank. If spelt correctly, it is Player 2's turn to roll the die.

If Player 1 misspelt the word, he or she makes corrections on the game board, and then erases it and writes the whole word again without looking at the Word Bank. If it is misspelt again the player erases it again and follows the same steps until it is correct.

Train Seats: A player may only write two words on each seat. The player who fills all five of their seats with words first is the winner. If a player rolls the number of a seat that already has two words in it, they may write the word in the Luggage Rack. If the Luggage Rack is also full, the player does not write a word and it is the other player's turn.

The Guard: If a player rolls number 6, they have opened the door to the Guard's Office. The Guard clears all the words from the Luggage Rack before they close the door. The Luggage Rack does not have to be full to win the game.

Winning

The player who fills all five of their seats with words first is the winner. If neither player has filled all the seats when time is up, the one with the most seats filled wins.

Fill the seats!

What is Letterland Phonics?

Letterland is a unique, phonics-based approach to teaching reading, writing and spelling to 3-8 year olds. Its characters make plain black letter shapes and their sounds easy and fun to remember. They give speedy access to **all 44 sounds and their major spellings**. They create fast, smooth transitions to blending plain letters to read, and segmenting spoken words to spell.

How does it work?

Sounds
Harry Hat Man makes the sound at the beginning of his name. Just whisper it – '*hhh...*'.

Shapes
Hurry from the Hat Man's head down to his heel on the ground.
Go up and bend his knee over, so he'll hop while he makes his sound.

Actions
Actions for each letter create strong multisensory cues for quickly learning and recalling letter shapes and sounds.

Uppercase
When Harry has a chance to start a name, he is so happy, he does a handstand with his hat on!

Digraphs
Whenever Sammy Snake starts to hiss loudly behind Harry Hat Man, the Hat Man turns back and says '**sh!**' because he hates noise.

Letterland activates every learning channel through simple phonics-related stories, actions, songs and activities.

1. **Learn letter sounds**

   Once you have met the friendly Letterland characters, just start to say their names for the correct letter sound.

2. **Learn letter shapes**

   Simple rhymes and songs about the Letterland characters ensure correct letter formation, avoiding confusion over similar looking letters.

3. **Word building**

   Blending and segmenting words is introduced very early on, covering blends, digraphs and trigraphs.

4. **Advanced spelling**

   Phonics stories give children a friendly logic for remembering all 44 letter sounds and their major spellings.

5. **Full literacy**

   Letterland takes children through from the very first foundation stages of learning to full literacy with a wide range of resources; from flashcards and software to decodable readers and handwriting resources. To find out more about the range, please visit our website: www.letterland.com

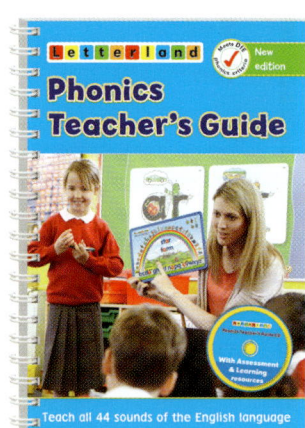

Scope of Letterland Phonics Teacher's Guide

Section 1: Fast Track - Phonemic Awareness

Teaching Focus:
- An alphabet immersion activity introducing all **a-z** shapes and their sounds
- Developing phonemic awareness of beginning sounds in words

Assessment Objective:
- Say the sound when shown the plain letter (21 consonants and 5 short vowels)
- Sort pictured words according to initial sound

Section 2: a-z Word Building

Teaching Focus:
- **a-z** letters in detail (uppercase/lowercase)
- First blending and segmenting (after six letters)
- Introducing long vowels while keeping the focus of Word Building on short vowels
- Common consonant digraphs: **ch ck sh th th ng**
- Introducing a limited number of 'tricky' words
- Practising decoding and reading 'tricky' words in brief, engaging stories

Assessment Objective:
- Say the sound(s) when shown the plain letter(s) for 21 consonants, 5 short and long vowels, 5 consonant digraphs
- Write the letter(s) in response to the sound
- Recognise uppercase and lowercase letter forms
- Blend and segment VC and CVC words
- Spell regular VC and CVC words accurately
- Read 21 'tricky' words
- Read decodable text with adequate comprehension

Section 3: Blending with Adjacent Consonants

Teaching Focus:
- Initial adjacent consonants:
  - sc sk sp st sm sn sw
  - bl cl fl gl pl sl
  - br cr dr fr gr pr tr
- Final adjacent consonants: **-st -sk -nd -nt -nk**

Assessment Objective:
- Blend and segment words of four sounds
- Read stories with adjacent consonant words
- Blend and segment CCVC and CVCC words
- Read 9 additional 'tricky' words (cumulative total: 30)
- Read decodable text containing adjacent consonants and 'tricky' words with accuracy, fluency and comprehension

Section 4: Long Vowels

Teaching Focus:
- **y** with long **i** sound (as in sk**y**)
  y with long **e** sound (as in bab**y**)
- Split digraphs: **a_e e_e i_e o_e u_e**
- Suffix: **ed** with three sounds /ed/ /d/ /t/
- Vowel digraphs: **ai ay ee ea ie oa ue**
- Long vowel spellings: **ind ild old**
- Blending and segmenting long vowel words
- Reading stories with long vowel words and also recognising 'tricky' words

Assessment Objective:
- Say the sound of split digraphs and long vowel digraphs when shown the plain letters
- Say three sounds for **y** and three for **-ed** when shown the plain letters
- Blend and segment words with long vowels
- Decode words with suffix **-ed**
- Read 17 new 'tricky' words (cumulative total: 47)
- Read decodable text containing long vowel words with accuracy, fluency and comprehension

Section 5: Further Vowel Sounds and Spellings

Teaching Focus:
- R-controlled vowels: **ar or er ir ur air ear**
- Long vowel patterns: **ow igh**
- Other vowel sounds: **oo oo u** (in push) **ou ow oi oy aw au ew**
- Reading stories with all the new sounds

Assessment Objective:
- Say the new sound when shown the letters
- Blend and segment words with the various vowel patterns and sounds
- Read 21 new 'tricky' words (cumulative total: 68)
- Apply the new sounds in reading with increasing accuracy, fluency and comprehension

Combining *Letterland Spelling* and *Letterland Phonics*

Letterland Spelling Teacher's Guide can be used in conjunction with the *Letterland Phonics Teacher's Guide* to cover all your curriculum requirements. Children may have already covered a lot of phonics in their reception year, but there are those who may be struggling to remember some of what they have covered. Finding a new way to present the information, using a new learning channel and engaging children with stories and characters, can be the key to successfully advancing the whole class.

The following pages give just the abbreviated stories about the Letterland characters and how they interact with each other to create a memorable way to learn and remember phonics. For full stories and teaching techniques please refer to the *Phonics Teacher's Guide* and accompanying product range.

Visit www.letterland.com for more details.

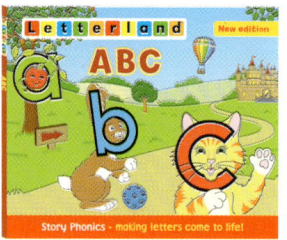
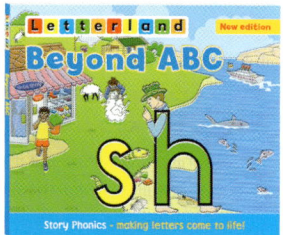
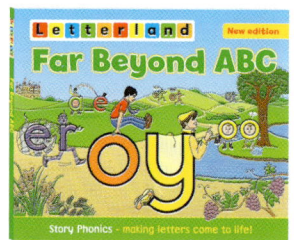
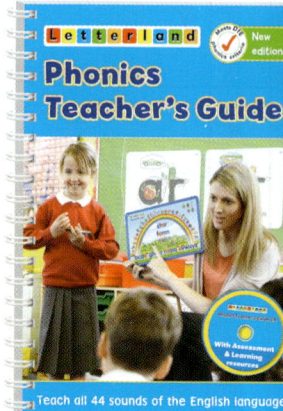

1: Hill Pass	ff		puff huff cuff	Firefighter Fred and his best friend Firefighter Frank both make their '**fff**' sound at the same time when they appear in words together.
	ll		bell tell hill	Lucy Lamp Light and her best friend, Linda Lamp Light, love making their '**lll**' sound together as they light up words with their lovely lemon-coloured light.
	ss		miss mess pass	Sammy Snake's best friend is his sister Sally. They love to make their hi**ss**ing sound together in words.
	zz		buzz fizzy	Zoe Zebra joins Zig Zag Zebra in words like bu**zz** and fi**zz**y.
2: Dock King	ck		duck pack sock	Clever Cat loves to sit safely just behind Kicking King, and watch while he ki**ck**s at the end of short, qui**ck** words.
	k		kit key kitten	Kicking King starts words like **k**it, **k**ey and **k**itten with his '**k**' sound.
3: Glove Catch	-ve		have live give	Vicky Violet makes sure that no Vase of Violets is in danger of falling over at the end of a word by putting a Silent Vase Prop **e** right beside it.
	-tch		chip chop much	When Clever Cat sits next to Harry Hat Man, his hairy hat tickles her nose and she almost always sneezes. Talking Tess remains silent.

4: Foxes Funny	-s	s	is was dogs	Sammy Snake sometimes has a little snooze and makes a sleepy 'zzz' sound instead of his usual hiss in words.
	-s	s	sun sand sad	Sammy Snake starts words like sun, sand and sad with his hissing 'sss' sound.
	-y	y	very family Andy Carly	Yellow Yo-yo Man works for Mr E at the end of thousands of words.
Pink Picnic	n	nk	pink	When Noisy Nick is behind Kicking King's back he doesn't make his usual sound. Instead he makes his singing sound.
6: Kicking Player	-ing	ing	making	This ending is exciting as it is a Magic Ending just as powerful as Magic e. Sparks jump back over one letter to make a Vowel Man appear and say his name.
	-er	er	later	Sometimes Ernest Er grabs a Magic e but he doesn't notice that the Magic Sparks can still reach over to make any Vowel Man appear and say his name.
7: Stopped Longer	-ed	ed	skated	In this ending both Eddy Elephant and Dippy Duck are saying 'ĕ' and 'd' as usual.
	-ed	ed	hoped baked chased	When both Eddy Elephant and Dippy Duck play the Disappearing Game both sounds disappear! Talking Tess is the only one who sees them disappearing. That is why we hear her 't' sound instead.
	-ed	ed	smiled waved closed	When Eddy Elephant plays the Disappearing Game in this ending, his sound disappears too.
The Quickest	-est	est	closest	This is a Magic Ending, just as powerful as Silent Magic e. The est ending means 'the most'.
9: Rainy Way	ai	ai	rain train tail	When Mr A and Mr I go out walking, Mr A does all the talking. He just says his name, 'A!' while Mr I remains silent, as he looks out for robots.
	ay	ay	say way stay	When Mr A and Yellow Yo-yo Man go out walking, Mr A does all the talking. He just says his name, 'A!' while Yellow Yo-yo Man remains silent, as he looks out for dangerous robots.

10: Lake Scene	a-e		make cape plane	Silent Magic **e** shoots back its magic sparks over one letter to make Mr A appear and say his name, '**A**!' in lots of words.
	e-e		these Pete delete	Silent Magic **e** shoots back its magic sparks over one letter to make Mr E appear and say his name, '**E**!' in just a few words.
11: Bike Zone	i-e		like fine size	Silent Magic **e** shoots back its magic sparks over one letter to make Mr I appear and say his name, 'Ī!', in lots of words.
	o-e		home hope rope	Silent Magic **e** shoots back its magic sparks over one letter to make Mr O appear and say his name, 'Ō!', in lots of words.
12: Huge Sheep	u-e		cube use	Silent Magic **e** shoots back its magic sparks over one letter to make Mr U appear and say his name, '**U**!', in a few words.
	ee		bee sleep week	When Mr E and his brother go out walking, Mr E does all the talking. He just says his name, '**E**!' But his brother remains silent, as he looks out for dangerous robots.
13: Beach Head	ea		sea beach read	When Mr E and Mr A go out walking, Mr E does all the talking. He just says his name, '**E**!' while Mr A remains silent, as he looks out for dangerous robots.
	ea		head ready weather	When Mr E and Mr A go out walking, Eddy Elephant may do the talking instead.
14: Field Farm	ie		believe field shield	When Mr I and Mr E go out walking, it may be Mr E's turn to do the talking.
	ar		farm car park	When you see an apple behind a robot's back you have already spotted Arthur Ar, the apple stealer! He reports back to his ringleader, Red Robot, with his last name, '**Ar**!'.
15: Herb Dinner	er		her faster mother	When you see an elephant behind a robot's back, you have already spotted Ernest Er, the Elephant Stealer! He reports back to his ringleader, Red Robot, with his last name, '**Er**!'.

16: Girls Surf	ir		girl shirt bird	When you see a bottle of ink behind a robot's back, you have already spotted Irving Ir, the Ink Stealer! He reports back to his ringleader, Red Robot, with his last name, '**Ir**!'.
	ur		fur burn turn	When you see an umbrella behind a robot's back, you have already spotted Urgent Ur, the Umbrella Stealer! He reports back to his ring leader, Red Robot, with his last name, '**Ur**!'.
17: Cool Book	oo		book look foot	When the Boot Twin takes the Foot Twin's boots and the Foot Twin accidentally steps in a puddle, he cries out, '**Oo**! Just l**oo**k at my f**oo**t!'
	u		put pull bush	When umbrellas get p**u**shed into their letter shapes upside down they don't make the usual sound.
18: Toad Toes	oa		boat coat goat	When Mr O and Mr A go out walking, Mr O does all the talking. He just says his name, '**Ō**!' while Mr A remains silent, as he looks out for dangerous robots.
	ow		show blow grow	Old Mr O stops Walter Walrus from teasing Oscar Orange by crying out '**Oh**!' so loudly that Walter is too surprised to make any sound at all.
20: Loud Town	ou		out house sound	When Walter Walrus fills Uppy Umbrella's letter with water and splashes Oscar Orange from there, Walter slips and and we hear them both sh**ou**ting '**Ou**!' (as in **ou**ch!).
	ow		how now crowd	Watch out when you see an orange next to Walter Walrus. When Walter splashes salty water in Oscars eyes, Walter also bumps his chin and they both h**ow**l, '**Ow**!'
21+22: Blue Crew	ue		hue	Occasionally Mr U and Mr E go out walking and Mr U does all the talking. He just says his name, '**U**!' while Mr E remains silent, as he looks out for dangerous robots.
	ew		few	Eddy Elephant knows Walter Walrus loves to tease. To stop him he squirts water right at him. Walter is so surprised he cries out, '**Oo**! **You**!'
23: Tie Bright	ie		tie cried pie	When Mr I and Mr E go out walking, Mr I usually does all the talking. He just says his name, '**Ī**!' while Mr E remains silent, as he looks out for dangerous robots.
	igh		night light right	When Mr I sees Golden Girl carefully being completely quiet next to Harry Hat Man, he often calls out '**Ī**!' and gives her an ice-cream for being so good.

24: Royal Soil	oy		boy toy joy	There's a boy called Roy in Letterland, who enjoys leaping over an 'o' into Yellow Yo-yo Mans sack. Roy shouts 'oy' as he leaps.
	oi		coin noise join	In a few words you will find Roy playing his game with Mr I. Then Mr I pretends to be annoyed, but they really both enjoy making a noise, 'oi!'
25: Short Shore	or		for horn north	When you see an orange behind a robot's back you have already spotted Orvil Or, the orange stealer! He reports back to his ringleader, Red Robot, with his last name, 'Or!'.
	ore		more	Orvil Or absorbs Magic e's sparks so he can still report back with his last name, 'Or!'
26: Naughty Hawk	au		cause pause launch	When Walter Walrus is feeling naughty, he fills Uppy Umbrella's letter with water and splashes Annie Apple from there. She cries out, 'Aw! Don't be naughty!'.
	aw		saw draw claw	When Walter Walrus is about he splashes Annie Apple with salty water. She cries out, 'Aw! Don't be so awful!'
27: Airport Near	air		fair hair chair	When you see Mr A and Mr I behind a robot's back you have caught that robot in the act. Now they are too upset to speak, and he puffs out, 'Air!' as he captures the pair.
	ear		year hear clear	When you see Mr E and Mr A behind a robot's back you have caught that robot in the act. As he captures these Vowel Men he pretends he has a deaf ear. So all we hear is him shouting out 'Ear!' at them.
28: Share Pears	are		beware scare square	Inside words sometimes Arthur Ar carefully snares both Annie Apple and an e in two sacks. But the letters are heavy so as he runs off with them he puffs out hot air.
	ear		pear bear	When you see Mr E and Mr A behind a robot's back you have caught that robot in the act. He puffs out lots of hot 'air' as they are a heavy pair.
29: Dolphin Whistle	ph		photo alphabet phone	Harry Hat Man makes Peter Puppy happy by taking his photograph. Harry Hat Man laughs quietly with his teeth on his lips, so his usual 'hhh' sound becomes a 'fff' sound.
	wh		when which why	When Walter Walrus finds Harry Hat Man standing ahead of him with his tall hat on Walter can't see. So he splashes his hat off. Harry is too surprised to speak.

What is Letterland Grammar?

The emphasis of *Letterland Grammar* is on the ways in which children's writing can be improved by using simple grammatical concepts. It is a journey of exploration. Giving a child an analogy they can relate to has always been the key to Letterland's success. In the same way as the Letterland characters help children to learn phonics and letter shapes, *Letterland Grammar* uses analogies to explain grammatical concepts.

Most children have travelled in cars or buses, travelled down different types of streets and seen lots of different types of buildings. They will have noticed road signs and may know that these tell the driver something about the road. If we relate this analogy to reading, we can describe stories as towns. Within those towns there are streets which we call sentences. The words we see are the buildings, and just as buildings are modified, extended or developed, so words can change with the addition of prefixes, suffixes and tenses. With *Letterland Grammar*, as a child is reading, they are encouraged to think of their finger as a car travelling along a street looking out for 'reading' signs along the way.

Letterland Grammar covers the statutory requirements laid out in the National Curriculum for English at Key Stage 1 (England) for both Year 1 and Year 2.

The structure of the guide is based on concepts rather than year group. This enables you to teach the concepts in a flexible way, and at the pace best suited to individual children and classes. The pages that follow give you a brief summary of the analogies used in *Letterland Grammar*. Just imagine your Spelling train pulling in at the Grammar town and link the programmes together!

Scope of Letterland Grammar Teacher's Guide

Unit & Chapter	Topic	Definition
1.1	Capital letter Full stop	A sign to show where a sentence starts. A sign to show where a sentence ends.
1.2	Question mark	A sign to show the end of a sentence that is a question.
1.3	Exclamation mark	A sign to show the end of a sentence. It indicates surprise, shock or excitement in direct speech.
1.4	Commas for lists	A sign used to separate items in a list or series.
1.5a	Apostrophe - possessive	A mark above the text before a final **s** to identify the owner of something.
1.5b	Apostrophe - contraction	A mark showing the place where one or more letters and their sounds have been deleted to shorten a word.
2.1	Conjunction - and	A 'joining word', used to link words, phrases or clauses in a sentence.
2.2	Coordinating conjunction	A 'joining word', used to join words, phrases or clauses that are of equal importance within a sentence.
	Subordinating conjunction	Used to link a main and a dependent clause.
2.3	Expanded noun phrase	A group of words that work together to give information about the noun.
2.4	Statements, questions exclamations, commands	Sentences which tell you something, end with a question mark, an exclamation mark, or tell you to do something.
3.1	Plural noun suffix	Suffixes (letters joined to the end of a word) that turn a noun, meaning one thing, into a noun meaning two or more things.
3.2	Suffixes added to verbs	Suffixes can be added to verbs with no change to the root verb. Verbs are words about 'doing' something.
3.3	Prefix	A group of letters joined to the beginning of a word to change its meaning.
3.4	Suffixes to form nouns	A group of letters joined to the end of a word (some change to the root word) to change its meaning and make a noun.
3.5	Compound noun	A noun that is made by joining two or more words, e.g. noun+noun, adjective+noun, verb+noun.
3.6/3.7	Suffixes to form adjectives	A group of letters joined to the end of a word to change its meaning and make an adjective.
3.8	Suffixes to form adverbs	A group of letters joined to the end of a word to change its meaning and make an adverb.
4.1	Present and past tense	The form of a verb that shows when something happens, past or present.
4.2	Present progressive and past tense	The form of a verb that shows a continuing action in the past or present, created by adding a form of the verb 'to be'.

Combining *Letterland Spelling* and *Letterland Grammar*

In the *Letterland Spelling Stations Teacher's Guide* you will cover some suffixes, prefixes and compound nouns. The aim of each lesson is to introduce the pattern and use Word Banks to embed those spellings in the minds of your students. To introduce grammatical concepts, such as suffixes and prefixes, you may find it useful to use the *Grammar Teacher's Guide* alongside your spelling programme.

The abbreviated stories of concepts you will encounter in the the Platform One *Spelling Stations Teacher's Guide* can be found below. For more information please visit www.letterland.com.

4: Foxes Family	**Plural noun suffix**	A suffix is like an extension added to the side of a house.	
6: Kicking Player 7: Stopped Longer	**Suffixes added to verbs**	A suffix is like an extension added to the side of a building. A verb is like a building where there are lots of things happening; like a factory, or office building.	
8: The Quickest	**Suffixes to form adjectives**	There are lots of different types of extensions to buildings, just as there are different suffixes.	
30: Unusual Sunset	**Prefix**	A prefix is like a porch that we add to the front of a house or building.	
	Compound noun	Like creating a large house by knocking two smaller houses together sometimes with a corridor (hyphen) between them.	

→ Move on to Platform Two